RAISING GREAT KIDS

WORKBOOK FOR PARENTS OF PRESCHOOLERS

Resources by Henry Cloud and John Townsend

Boundaries
Boundaries Workbook
Boundaries audio
Boundaries video curriculum
Boundaries with Kids
Boundaries with Kids Workbook
Boundaries with Kids audio
Changes That Heal (Cloud)
Changes That Heal Workbook (Cloud)
Changes That Heal audio (Cloud)
Hiding from Love (Townsend)
The Mom Factor
The Mom Factor Workbook
The Mom Factor audio
Raising Great Kids
Raising Great Kids Workbook for Parents of Preschoolers
Raising Great Kids audio
Safe People
Safe People Workbook
Safe People audio
Twelve "Christian" Beliefs That Can Drive You Crazy

RAISING GREAT KIDS

A COMPREHENSIVE GUIDE TO

Parenting with Grace and Truth

WORKBOOK FOR PARENTS OF PRESCHOOLERS

AGES 0–5

Dr. Henry Cloud & Dr. John Townsend

with Lisa Guest

MOTHERS OF
MOPS.
PRESCHOOLERS

ZondervanPublishingHouse

Grand Rapids, Michigan

A Division of HarperCollinsPublishers

Raising Great Kids Workbook for Parents of Preschoolers
Copyright © 1999 by Henry Cloud and John Townsend

Requests for information should be addressed to:

 ZondervanPublishingHouse
Grand Rapids, Michigan 49530

ISBN 0-310-22571-X

Published in association with Yates and Greer, LLP, Literary Agent, Orange, CA

Interior design by Laura Klynstra

Printed in the United States of America

99 00 01 02 03 04 05 06 /❖ DC/ 10 9 8 7 6 5 4 3 2

Contents

Foreword to *Raising Great Kids*

At MOPS International—an organization that encourages and supports mothers of young children—we are often asked what resource we recommend on the elusive and challenging subject of parenting.

Well, here it is!

With all the fantastic books and curriculums available today, how can we choose *Raising Great Kids* as our favorite? Three reasons:

First, it works. It speaks the language moms and dads speak. It makes sense. We can *get* this stuff. When I consider the everydayness of parenting, Drs. Henry Cloud and John Townsend provide principles and techniques that work.

Second, it's biblical. With both theological and psychological training to their credit, the authors offer us an integrated and trustworthy perspective. They've done their homework and offer us the results.

Third, it's foundational. This big-picture book covers all the ages and stages of parenting while underlining the unique importance of the early years. As parents, it's great to begin with the end in mind. I can see the results of this parenting approach played out in the character of my own kids. No, they're not perfect. But they are great!

Take this moment from just a few weeks ago as an example.

Our family pushed our chairs back from the iron deck table where we had just consumed my daughter's favorite dinner of grilled chicken, pasta, and veggies. My husband and twelve-year-old son, Ethan, headed out to hit golf balls, leaving the summer evening stretching before fourteen-year-old Eva and me. We lingered on the deck, reviewing her excursions of the past three weeks: summer camp followed by a trip with her church youth group. I missed her.

My daughter, five feet eight inches, is growing up and away. I marvel at the young woman before me. To my surprise, that night she talks—really talks—with me about her life, touching on everything from boys to girlfriends to God. In one moment I recognize a gentle shift between us. Yes, I am still Mom. But I am becoming Friend. She still needs me, but differently than in the past decade. Our relationship nudges forward to a new place. Instinctively I know my daughter has now completed her childhood journey and now sets out in the direction of adulthood. Building on the parenting of her past, she reaches out and around me toward tomorrow. And I watch, amazed.

I remember her bouncy, two-year-old dimpled face, her eager excitement at five, her charming and willing spirit at ten, and her metamorphosis into adolescence just a year later. Now, sitting on the deck, enjoying her teen discoveries, I muse that our bonded relationship, forged in infancy and continuing to change, remains the single most important ingredient in our mother-daughter journey together. Sure, there were "looks" and spankings and time-outs and lectures that helped make her what she is today. But on this summer evening, at this juncture, I sit back in my deck chair, listen to my daughter, and recognize within me the peace of time well spent in a relationship. The nurture of my touch, my eyes focused on her eyes, my ears tuned to her voice, my investment in her from infancy forward are paying off.

So, as the president of MOPS International and as the mother of two growing and going children, I believe this book is the best resource for guiding us through the parenting process from rocking chair to deck chair. Whether you're just beginning your parenting journey, like many mothers of preschoolers, or well down the road, there is help for you here.

ELISA MORGAN
PRESIDENT AND CEO,
MOTHERS OF PRESCHOOLERS (MOPS), INC.

Dear Reader

Thanks for opening up this *Raising Great Kids Workbook*. We are excited about this workbook, and we hope you will find it helpful in your parenting. To make your experience a meaningful one, we wanted to begin by sharing a few of our thoughts about this resource.

We wrote this book with MOPS International (Mothers of Preschoolers), a Christian service organization that supports mothers and mothering with a worldwide network of local groups, speakers, and resources. We support their values and the work they do in helping so many moms survive and grow in their mothering years.

Also, we wanted to let you know our own passion behind the book. The first few years of life are the most critical period of growth and development for everyone. Infants start the process of trusting the love of Mom and Dad and God, toddlers begin experiencing freedom and responsibility, and children start understanding how to function in the real world. In short, this is a period in which a child's soul is developed.

As a parent, you are right at the center of this process. It is impossible to overestimate how important a role you play in rearing a child. As the Bible teaches, God shows us how to trust in him "even at my mother's breast" (Psalm 22:9). But most parents feel overwhelmed by the complexity of the job. With so many things to worry about, how do you know the real tasks and goals? Many parents become discouraged or don't know where to start.

We wrote *Raising Great Kids* to help with this problem. The book is a comprehensive resource that provides a structure for approaching parenting. It provides a road map for creating *character* in your children—the ability to function as God designed them to function in the world. The biblical principles apply to all ages and stages of kids, so you can use them as a guide for all the years you parent. We have provided lots of examples, illustrations, and suggestions to help you apply the information.

The organization of *Raising Great Kids* differs in a major way from this workbook. The book itself is not arranged by age. By design, we have included no infancy, toddler, school-age, or teen sections. Instead, we have organized the material by principles universal to all stages of parenting. For example, the character trait of connectedness applies to the infant who is learning to reach out for Mother's love as well as to the teenager who is attempting to connect not only to her parents but also to safe people in the outside world. By organizing the material in this fashion, we hope you will be able to see what your child needs in order to develop these character traits at any age and then help provide it for her. Also, this approach solves the old problem of the tendency to read only the sections of the book that apply to your kid.

However, we designed the workbook differently. We have planned three separate workbooks: this one dealing with infants and toddlers, one dealing with school-age kids, and one dealing with teens. A workbook is just what its name says: a book that helps you work in a practical, hands-on manner to apply principles to your specific situation. So we wanted to tailor this product in a more applicable manner for you. We hope your work is good work, the kind God completes in you (Philippians 1:6). And we pray that God will use it to help your parenting be the successful and worthwhile relationship he designed it to be.

We appreciate your labors as a parent. Happy reading, and God bless you!

HENRY CLOUD, PH.D.
JOHN TOWNSEND, PH.D.

How to Use This Workbook

The *Raising Great Kids Workbook* is designed to be used in a variety of ways.

- You will get the most out of your investment of time if you read *Raising Great Kids* as you work through this book. The text fleshes out key concepts with real-life examples and a more thorough discussion.
- You or you and your spouse—or you and a friend—can use the workbook on your own. In tandem with the text, the questions in this workbook will help you become more intentional and more effective in your parenting.
- You or you and your spouse can be part of a small group that meets regularly to discuss the challenges of parenting, share tips, and pray for each other and for your children.
- Key questions for parents of preschoolers are marked with the hand icon. Read all the questions in each chapter so that you follow the logic and understand the context of any given question. But let this icon help you focus on the most crucial questions for your specific situation. If you are reading *Raising Great Kids* with a group, the icon may help you choose which questions to discuss.
- Whether you're tackling *Raising Great Kids* on your own, with a spouse or another parent, or in a group, be sure to include plenty of prayer time. After all, whatever the age of our kids and whatever parenting challenges we currently face, we all need God to shore up the areas in which we are lacking skills, knowledge, or energy.

May God bless you as, with his guidance, you raise a great kid.

Introduction
A Forbidden Topic

Parenting Principles

- Relationship is central not only to the order of the universe God has created, but also to parenting.
- The Bible as well as our own observation tells us that, most of all, children need love.
- Love is essential, but love alone is not enough. We must have the structure of reality and truth to make relationships and the rest of life work well.
- Parenting is a long-term job, but one day children will have to go off on their own. After they have gone, the character their parents built into them will guide them.
- Character is never complete without an understanding of who one is before God. Healthy people have the ability to see who God is, to love him, to obey him, and to take their proper role under him.

Perhaps you've noticed for yourself that, in conversations about parenting philosophies and practices, battle lines are often drawn. Parenting is no safer a topic than politics and religion.*

- Some people advocate structure and control at the expense of everything else: to raise an obedient child is the most important thing. Others advocate love over structure: having a child feel loved and secure in love is primary.

---

*The parts in italics are passages from the book *Raising Great Kids*. Page references to *Raising Great Kids* are in parentheses.

Some people emphasize the sinfulness of children while others talk about the inherent goodness and innocence of children.

— As you begin working through the *Raising Great Kids Workbook*, what do you see as a parent's primary job? Put differently, what is your parenting philosophy? Which of the four groups mentioned above (if any) comes closest to verbalizing your perspective and priorities?

— Having considered your philosophy on parenting, now briefly explain why you picked up this book. What do you hope to learn? What kind of help are you looking for?

• People's conversation about parenting philosophies and practices becomes impassioned because it is conversation about their children's welfare, their community, their own welfare, and their God—four aspects of their lives in which they invest their very hearts.

— What specific aspects of your child's welfare are you most concerned about? List the top four or five here. (Doesn't merely writing them down get your heart beating faster?)

— What admonitions about parenting from people in your community do you carry around internally? When have you wanted to disagree with some of the advice you have received? If you bucked that advice, what happened? What risks to relationships are involved in your efforts to parent the way you believe best for your child?

— Give two or three examples of how your life (your own welfare) is greatly affected by how your young child is doing. Then imagine a few examples that probably await you in the future. How, for instance, could a child's choice of friends, willingness (or unwillingness) to study, and decisions about sex or spirituality affect you?

— When have you realized that a discussion of parenting styles is in fact a discussion of religion? How does your relationship with God impact your parenting both theoretically and practically?

All around the country, parents are discussing parenting philosophies and practices. They feel tremendous pressure to do the right thing for their child, for themselves, in light of their community, and before God. It's a daunting task. To help you in this task, we have built this book around some of the values that are most important to us. Let's look at some of these now before you go through the book.

The Value of Love (page 14)

Relationship is central not only to the order of the universe God has created, but also to parenting. You, a parent, can't construct character in children without having a deep relationship with each one of them.

• The Bible as well as our own observation tells us that, most of all, children need love. Not only is relationship central for their development, but it is their ultimate goal in life as well. Furthermore, Jesus himself summed up the entire Jewish law in the simple statement "Love God and love others." That's why a relational system lies at the core of this book.

— What experiences in your childhood taught you that you were loved— or made you feel unloved and perhaps even unlovable?

— What can you learn from your own growing-up years that will help you teach your children the value of love?

Your children need to be deeply related to you and others, and you are going to have to keep relationship as a goal of their development. We will help you do that all along the way.

The Value of Truth (page 15)

Love is essential, but love alone is not enough. We must have the structure of reality and truth to make our relationships and the rest of life work well.

- Children cannot be loved too much, but they can be disciplined not enough.

    — What kind of discipline (or lack of discipline) did you grow up with? What were the results, good and/or bad?

    — Parents are dispensers of truth and reality sometimes through direct teaching, sometimes through discipline, and sometimes by getting out of the way and letting consequences do the instructing. What lessons of truth and reality did your parents teach most effectively? Which of these three methods do you remember them using—and at what point of your life?

    — Again, what can you learn from your own growing-up years that will help you teach your children the value of truth?

Parents want each of their children to become a person of truth, living in wisdom. In the following pages we have tried to show you what kinds of truth children need at what ages and how to present it to them.

The Role of Character (page 15)

Parenting is a temporary job. One day your children will have to go off on their own. After they have gone, the character you built into them will guide them.

- As a parent you need to be much more concerned about what kind of tree (good or bad) your child is becoming than about any particular fruit you might see on a single day.

  — Is this statement challenging or freeing or, to some degree, both? Explain your answer.

  — At this introductory point, what does the word "character" mean to you? What thoughts and questions come to mind as you consider building character into your children?

In this book we have always tried to see a particular problem or task in light of the ultimate task of character development so that you can be more concerned about the tree rather than only the behavioral fruit of the day. We want to help you to have not only children who obey, but also children who become people who obey. Anyone can obey with a police officer around, but ultimately only people of character obey when no one is around to tell them what to do. So we'll define "character" and instruct you how to develop it in your children.

An Understanding of Sin, Immaturity, and the Image of God (page 16)

We believe, first, that children are created in the image of God and have a lot of good things about them from the start. Second, children are sinners, and all of their goodness is affected by sin. Third, children do not show up already assembled; they are immature and must be "put together" by the parenting process.

- These three beliefs lead us to assert that everything a child does is not necessarily bad, or good, or immature. You have to discern which is which. Furthermore, you can't judge a behavior, in and of itself, out of context of character. Consider these two examples. First, two preschool girls may manifest similar needy and clingy behavior on a given day. One girl's mother, however, may be away on an extended trip. The other girl's mother is home, but she has, in her parenting, subtly punished independence and rewarded clinginess. The first behavior is neediness; the second, manipulation. As another example, two three-year-old boys both say *no* when Mom says, "Time for a nap." The first might be simply protesting and defining himself, but he knows he is going to bed. The second may be saying *no* because he has learned that he can do whatever he wants in his house; he is not planning to go to bed at all.

  — Give another example or two of the kinds of behavior that might mean either neediness or manipulation. What behaviors might be the image of God manifesting itself (good assertiveness) or disobedience (sinful rebellion)?

  — At this point of your parenting, what kinds of clues do you think might help you determine what is motivating your child's behavior at a particular moment?

It is important to give what they need to immature children who are incomplete. It is important to discipline children who rebel against truth, you, God, and structure. It is important to nurture the very potential God built into them.

The Value of Freedom (page 17)

God created humankind to grow into self-control (Galatians 5:23). So it is important for you to play a role in your children's lives that will help them gain control of themselves and their own lives.

- We also believe that freedom undergirds everything God has for people (Galatians 5:1) and that this freedom is to be used responsibly in the service of love.

  — What kinds of freedoms did you grow up with? Give examples from different points in your childhood. What kinds of responsibility did your parents require of you at those specific points in time? Comment on the balance they maintained between freedom and responsibility. (Was it effective and reasonable? Did it help you mature, or did it hinder that process?)

  — In what ways, if any, did your parents prepare you for eventually taking control of your own life? (Does a certain conversation with one of them or one of their pet phrases stand out in your mind?) What can you learn from your experience and apply to your parenting?

We will help you to not fear the freedom of your children, but at the same time to require responsibility from them.

The Role of God (page 17)

Character is never complete without an understanding of who one is before God. Healthy people have the ability to see who God is, to love him, to obey him, and to take their proper role under him.

- God gave parents the assignment of bringing up children to love and be in relationship with him and, eventually, to take their proper place in life as his children (Deuteronomy 6:20–25).

— Did your parents fulfill this God-given assignment? If so, what did they do? What can you learn from what they did right (or wrong) in this regard?

— What would you have liked to have received from your parents in the way of spiritual training and guidance? How will you teach your own children those very things?

We want to help you help your children understand God and his values and their role before him. We also want to help you help them understand God's love and his ways. So this will be another thread throughout the book.

The Process (page 18)

Parenting is a process that begins with conception or adoption and ends many years later. What you need to do as a parent will change every day. But once you understand the principles involved, you will be more likely to do the right thing and enjoy raising great kids.

• What advantages do you see to an exposition of principles rather than a book organized according to chronological development?

• What specific issues involving the parenting of toddlers and preschoolers do you hope to learn about in the following pages? Watch for and consider those as you learn the parenting principles you will find here.

We have written this book with process in mind, with a focus on the necessary ingredients and tasks of parenting no matter what your child's age. Where age-specific interventions are needed, we have provided you with maps and instructions. But most important, we want you to have guidelines no matter where you find yourself in the process, from infancy to college.

Godspeed (page 19)

Parents want to do the right thing, and they can—given the right help. We hope you will find this book to be one of the many helps you will need along the way.

- Carefully consider three of our main points:

  1. Balance the role of love with the need for limits.
  2. Value the worth of children without turning them into little gods.
  3. Children have much potential, but need a lot of both nurturing and correction to achieve that.

  — Which of these points of instruction do you expect to have the easiest time following?

  — Which one will be most challenging? Why? What might you do to improve your chances for success in that area?

- Ultimately, we believe in God's plan for parenting as outlined in the principles of the Bible. We don't, however, believe in a particular, rigid way of following those principles.

  — What biblical principles come to mind that can serve as guidelines for your parenting?

— What biblical truths have you come to appreciate more as you have grown and have observed more of how the world functions? Let your own experience reinforce the value of following God's ways in every aspect of your life, including your parenting.

• Most parents wonder what to do when their infant cries. The fact is, you can't spoil an infant. A baby who cries is not trying to manipulate you, but is expressing a need to reach out to something bigger than himself. When you hold and comfort your baby, the child is internalizing your love. That message becomes part of the fabric of his soul and establishes the kind of dependency that will allow him to be not only in relationship with others, but ultimately in relationship with God. Starting at around 12 months of age, that child should hopefully have internalized enough love to be able to experience gradually the reality that life has limits. Over time, he now needs to learn to tolerate some waiting, frustration, and ultimately responsibility and consequences, as he has the ability to bear them.

Pray hard, get lots of support, implement what we suggest, and enjoy the trip. And may God be with you each and every step along the way as you raise some great kids!

Hands-on Exercise

If You Do One Thing Besides Pray . . .

Before getting into the material more deeply, pause to summarize what you hope to learn and list any specific questions you have about parenting your young child. You can refer to this page along the way to make sure you're learning what you want to learn and then, at the end, to see what God has shown you about the quite daunting, but extremely rewarding call to parent.

Folded-Hands Exercise

"My help comes from the LORD . . ."

—PSALM 121:2

Lord God, the chapter's closing statement—both a charge and a benediction—reinforces what I already know: I need you in my efforts to parent the child you have entrusted to me. You have blessed me in some amazing ways throughout my life, but never with a gift as precious as this child. And I've had some tough stewardship issues along the way, but nothing like this. Parenting will keep me on my knees praying hard. It will compel me to find support. So I thank you that you are a faithful and loving God. Please show me where to go and whom to lean on. The challenges of raising this child will invite me to try different things: Lord, give me discernment and creativity as I look for ways to help my child become a person of godly character. And, since the journey is a long one, Lord, please help me sense your guiding and empowering presence with me so that I might enjoy the trip. I'm thankful that you will be with me every step of the way, redeeming my mistakes, guiding my efforts, and blessing my attempts to raise my child to live a life that pleases and glorifies you. I pray in Jesus' name. Amen.

Part One

Raising Children of Character

One

The Goal of Parenting
A Child with Character

Parenting Principles

- The parent's task is to develop a little person into an adult. The issue along the way is not about being good, but about having good character.
- Character is the sum of our abilities to deal with life as God designed us to.
- As a child grows up, parents transfer more and more freedom and responsibility from their shoulders to their child's.
- Growing character in children always involves the elements of development and internalizing.

Everybody wants good kids. Good children do what they're supposed to do, so this is a proper and right desire. The issue is not about merely being good because many good children don't grow up handling life well. They may become either not-so-good people or good, but immature, adults. As my friend Tony learned, the issue is not about being good, but about having good character (pages 23–24).

The Importance of Being a Parent (page 24)

If you are a parent, you are engaged in one of the most meaningful jobs in the world. You are doing eternally significant work: developing a little person into an adult.

- What routine and mundane aspects of the huge and relentless task of parenting often keep you from being focused on the eternal significance of your work?

• What helps—or could help—you keep your eyes on the big picture and ultimate goal of parenting between episodes of spilled milk and arguments about dirty rooms?

Once you've become a parent, it can be hard to get your head above water long enough to figure out exactly what you are trying to accomplish and how you will know when you get there. Parents need a way to keep in mind the ultimate goal of parenting: creating an adult.

Creating an Adult (page 25)

We parents define success not by how our child is doing today, but by what happens after she leaves home.

• What hopes for your child-as-adult do you have for the following aspects of her life?

— School

— Job

— Dating

— Marriage

— Friendships

— Personal values and conduct

— Spiritual life

- One of the elements of childhood is dependency, but God designed your child to function independently of you one day. You are investing in helping your child leave you.

  — Consider the very real parent-wounds that moms and dads suffer as their child grows up and then eventually leaves. What do you think makes those moments you listed and that eventuality painful, or bittersweet?

  — What can you learn (or have you learned) from moms and dads you've seen experience that parent-wound and deal well with the pain? What source(s) of strength and comfort did they draw on? What groundwork did they lay early in their parenting years for dealing with that hurt which means success?

Sadly, kids don't always grow up well. Sometimes they don't leave, and they depend on their parents far too long. At other times they leave, but they aren't prepared for adult life. They are adults on the outside, but they are broken or undeveloped on the inside.

Who Is Responsible for What? (page 26)

Who is responsible for your child's maturity and readiness for the world? You or your child? We believe in the following three principles about responsibility.

1. Responsibility lies on a continuum between child and parent, and its position on the continuum changes over time. The child's only responsibility at the beginning of life is to need and take in the sources of life, such as love; parents have total responsibility for the child.

— What behaviors or attitudes have already suggested that your child is moving away from this end of the continuum?

— What do you find helpful about this idea that the amount or kind of responsibility a child has lies on a continuum? How does this image help you approach the task of parenting?

2. Even though responsibility shifts, both parents and children have their own unique and distinct tasks. Parents and children can't do each other's jobs; they must do their own.

— What are you doing to provide safety and love for your child (your tasks as a parent)?

— What experiences can you structure to help your preschooler take on greater responsibility? For example, what kind of schedule and system of rules for doing chores and what consequences for not doing them could you establish?

— The child's tasks are to take risks, fail, and learn lessons. What risks have you seen your young one take? How have you—or how do you want to—respond to your child's risk taking and failures?

3. Children must bear the ultimate responsibility for their lives.

— What seeds of this truth can a parent sow during a child's early years? What will you do, for instance, to stay emotionally connected to your child while keeping good limits with her? Instead of retracting the consequence (keeping good limits), what do you say, for example, when your heartbroken child has temporarily lost a much-loved toy to time out because he misused it (staying emotionally connected)?

— What, if anything, did you learn before first grade about the fact that you are ultimately responsible for your life?

While your children are coming to terms today with what are their tasks and what are not, they always need to be moving toward full responsibility for their life and soul.

Your Parenting Reflects Your Goals (page 27)

Ironically, we often know our financial and career goals more clearly than we do our childrearing goals.

• As a parent of a young child, you have many fires to put out, and today's worries keep you busy enough. But take a moment now and indicate which of the following goals your parenting at this point reflects.

Survival	Independence/self-sufficiency
Competence	Problem solving
Morality	Religious life

• Now consider the list again as well as any other possibilities. What goal(s) would you like your parenting to reflect? What changes might you have to make for that to happen?

My friend Tony wanted his daughter Halley to be a good kid. Good kids are a product of the real goal of parenting: mature character. When children grow up with mature character, they are able to take their place as adults in the world and function properly in all areas of life. Character growth is the main goal of child rearing.

Character: The Real Goal (page 29)

But what is character?

- Who among your friends and acquaintances would you describe as a person of good character? List two or three people.

- For some, *character* means having integrity, being responsible, and standing for the right thing. We, however, view character as the structures and abilities within ourselves that make up how we operate in life. In other words, character is *the sum of our abilities to deal with life as God designed us to.*

  — Consider the people of character you listed above in light of this broader definition. What "abilities to deal with life" do their lives reflect?

  — Now consider specific ways to give your child "abilities to deal with life." When your toddler is frightened, for example, hold and soothe her so that she learns that love is available, but that she needs to reach out for it.

- You may know adults who look good and perform well, but who have character flaws (a bad temper, a tendency to withdraw, or self-centeredness) that diminish their life experience. More often than not, these flaws began in childhood and continued on in life.

  — Which of your own character flaws have their roots in your childhood? Explain.

— What lessons in character do you wish you had learned when you were young?

— What might you do to teach your child those lessons you missed? Be specific.

When you help your child develop character, you are addressing the heart of parenting. Character provides a tool kit of spiritual and emotional skills that prepare a child to succeed in life.

The Aspects of Character (page 31)

What does character in a child look like? In Part 2 we will explain in detail the six distinct aspects of character, but we will start thinking about each aspect now, through the two questions that appear with the list below.

- **Attachment:** the ability to form relationships

  (1) What did your parents do right (or wrong) to help you develop this character trait?

  (2) What is one thing you might do now to help your child develop this aspect of character?

- **Responsibility:** taking ownership of one's life and seeing it as one's own problem

  (1) What did your parents do right (or wrong) to help you develop this character trait?

  (2) What is one thing you might do now to help your child develop this aspect of character?

- **Reality:** the ability to accept the negatives of the real world

   (1) What did your parents do right (or wrong) to help you develop this character trait?

   (2) What is one thing you might do now to help your child develop this aspect of character?

- **Competence:** the development of everyday life skills as well as one's God-given gifts and talents

   (1) What did your parents do right (or wrong) to help you develop this character trait?

   (2) What is one thing you might do now to help your child develop this aspect of character?

- **Conscience:** an internal sense of right and wrong

   (1) What did your parents do right (or wrong) to help you develop this character trait?

   (2) What is one thing you might do now to help your child develop this aspect of character?

- **Worship:** learning that God loves her and is in charge of life; learning to seek God on her own

   (1) What did your parents do right (or wrong) to help you develop this character trait?

   (2) What is one thing you might do now to help your child develop this aspect of character?

It is important to note here that these character aspects are attributes of God's own character. The difference is that, while God has always had these character traits, your child is in the process of developing them. Your first, last, and best goal is to be a good agent of developing mature character within your child's life and soul.

How Character Is Developed (page 32)

Growing your children's character always involves two elements: development, *training through experience and practice; and* internalizing, *taking those experiences inside to become a part of their personality.*

- Teaching transfers information from one to another. But teaching alone doesn't make the child "own," or take responsibility for, the information. We learn and grow from what we engage in. You can't learn how to ride a bicycle from just reading a book—you have to get on a bike. What is one lesson you learned "the hard way" (by engaging in it or, put differently, through experience) as you were growing up?

- In teaching or developing character, you will provide a wealth of experiences to help your child engage in and learn about realities such as relationship, responsibility, and forgiveness.

  — What has your child learned about relationships even at her young age? What, for instance, have the times you've left her with a baby-sitter and then come back to her taught her about her relationship with Mom and Dad—about attachment (the ability to form relationships), reality (accepting the negatives of the real world), your reliability, and so on?

  — What can your child's experience in misplacing his favorite blanket teach about responsibility?

— What realities have the consequences of her behavior taught your young child? Give two or three examples. Let the parents' mantra "You don't get what you want when you cry" start your list!

While it's important to teach your child about loving and being loved and about taking responsibility (Deuteronomy 6:20–25), information is never enough. Your child needs many, many experiences in which he sees reality and adapts to it—or suffers the consequences of ignoring it.

How to Know What to Develop (page 35)

It is easy to be overwhelmed by the complexity of character development. You must deal with several character aspects at once; you don't have the option of working on one issue until it is resolved and then moving to the next. Your child needs to be growing in each area continuously, but with different tasks appropriate to his level of maturity as he grows.

• What experiences could help your preschooler learn the reality that the people who gratify him are the same ones who frustrate him? Being loving and attentive while you enforce a consequence for misbehavior can, for instance, help your child with this task.

• What areas of competence is your toddler or preschooler working on mastering?

• What seeds for her spiritual growth are you sowing in your young child's life? Which seem to be taking root? Cite evidence.

This book will provide a road map you can use to further evaluate where your child is in the major character areas—attachment, responsibility, reality, competence, morality, and worship/spiritual life.

Fruits and Roots (page 36)

When you understand and interact with your child on a character level, you will quickly find that what seems to be a problem isn't really the problem. After all, you can't see or touch character. What you can see is how your child responds to life.

- Your child's behavior, attitudes, and emotions serve as an indicator light about character issues. Through observation you will know better how to provide growth experiences tailored to help your child mature and develop in a particular area.

— What character issues might biting and throwing tantrums point to: a lack of attachment? an inability to sense responsibility for the consequences of one's actions? something else?

— What could a parent do to address the real issues behind such toddler behaviors? What limits could be set and what consequences enforced? Then, what could be done to eliminate that behavior?

- Effective parents look for what a symptom reveals about their child's struggle to grow up. These parents then help their child deal with the root problem.

— Why is this a tough assignment?

— Why is this approach crucial to the development of good character?

Now that you have the big-picture goal of parenting as character building, the next two chapters will explain the ingredients God has provided that help parents produce growth toward character in children: grace, truth, and time.

Hands-on Exercise

If You Do One Thing Besides Pray . . .

Make a point of regularly talking to your child about his or her day. Then, if you are able to put her experience into your own words, she will feel that you empathically "get" what she is saying. Attachment—a key element of character—will be happening.

Folded-Hands Exercise

"My help comes from the LORD . . ."

—PSALM 121:2

Thank you, Lord, for entrusting my children to my care. What a gift each one is—and what an awesome responsibility! I thank you that you love my children even more than I do and that you are there for me as I approach this task and privilege of parenting. Please, God, guide me as I sow seeds of attachment, responsibility, reality, competence, morality, and a spiritual life that glorifies you—and then, Lord, please protect and grow those seeds to fruition! I pray in Jesus' name. Amen.

— Two —

The Ingredients of Grace and Truth

Parenting Principles

- Parents need to show children grace, to show them that they are for them.
- Parents need to give children truth, to give them reality and necessary limits.
- Grace helps children tolerate dealing with truth.

Did Dan and Karen's conversation sound familiar (pages 38–39)? Do you and your spouse frequently find yourselves on different sides of the argument when you need to decide between "cutting some slack" or enforcing the limits? Or, even more common, do you find yourself at odds with yourself on this issue?

Grace and Truth Divided (page 39)

The ingredients we need as we parent our children toward character growth—grace and truth—are separate and different elements. Choosing between the two is not the problem. Getting them together is. An effective parent must learn to be gracious and truthful at the same time.

Consider the two ingredients:

1. Your children need to know that you are on their side. You do this by showing them empathy. That is an expression of grace, or favor, and this grace is an environment the parent provides that allows growth. As grace is taught and modeled, as parents let their child know that "we are for you," grace is experienced and internalized by the child.
2. Your children need to know that you will give them reality and set necessary limits, and that is truth. Truth is in accord with God's standards,

the timeless realities he wove into his creation. Truth is the state of being reliable and trustworthy.

- Turn to pages 40–41 in the text and look again at the lists of forms and qualities in which grace and truth manifest themselves.

— Which group do you tend to practice more easily than the other? Why do you think that comes more easily?

— What do you think keeps you from offering the other to your child? What might you do to overcome or remove those barriers?

- Grace and truth need to come together in our parenting. During a child's temper tantrum, for instance, the parent needs to stay emotionally connected to the child even though he is behaving badly. At the same time, the parent needs to hold to the truth, to the standard that the behavior is in fact unacceptable.

— As you've parented your two- or three-year-old, when have you noticed that you are struggling to get grace and truth together? You may, for instance, find yourself becoming angry when your child repeatedly ignores your instruction to pick up her toys rather than allowing consequences, not your anger, to train her.

— In one of the situations you just identified, what could you have done to be gracious and truthful at the same time?

— Now be specific about a situation or two in your home where grace and truth have come together for you as you parent.

Your child is young, but it's not too early for you to begin thinking about how to bring grace and truth together in your parenting. In fact, depending on how you were raised, you may be struggling to get them together for yourself. (Remember the possible paths Dan and Karen's son Jason could take?) Most of us can identify with some aspect of feeling divided between grace and truth.

Integration (page 42)

One goal of parenting is to integrate grace and truth. From the earliest days on, parents must at the same time love their children and provide limits and structures. They must be loving and firm. They must be kind, but require their children to do their part. They must be compassionate and forgiving, but require the children to change and be responsible.

- A rule of thumb for integrating grace and truth is "Be soft on the person, but hard on the issue."

  — As you were growing up, when (if ever) were your parents soft on you but hard on the issue? Give details about the situation and about your response to their parenting in that moment.

  — In what typical parenting situation (such as not coming the first time she is called, not sitting at the dinner table through the meal) could this rule of thumb clarify your role or help you formulate your words to your child? Be specific.

- As you try to live out the rule of thumb "Be soft on the person, but hard on the issue," remember that grace establishes and maintains the quality of the relationship, and truth adds direction for the growth and structure of a child's behavior and performance.

— Earlier you identified which is easier for you to offer your child: grace or truth. Look again (page 43 in the text) at how Dan and Karen each added the missing ingredient to their parenting. Below list two or three statements appropriate for a parenting situation you frequently face. Be sure that they reflect the addition of either grace or truth to your parenting.

— Consider now the child's perspective. What is helpful in a practical sense about this balance between grace and truth? Why does this balance improve the relationship as well as the behavior?

- As children grow, your expression of grace and truth needs to change. At different ages, children need different kinds of kindness and structure. But the formula is the same: grace and truth must go together.

— Turn to the chart on pages 43–47 and find the age of your preschooler (Infancy, Toddlerhood, or Childhood). What, if anything, surprises you about what you found in the Grace category? in the Truth category?

— What do the statements listed in the columns of Grace and Truth show you about your parenting—your strengths as well as your weaknesses?

— What makes sense to you about the balance of grace and truth as presented for a child the age of your own?

Whether you are parenting a toddler or a collegian, the formula is the same. Both grace and truth need to be in the mix. Few parents would subscribe to just one of those ingredients (just one of the columns in the chart), but many parents end up operating out of primarily one column. For children to develop character, they need to be given grace and *truth in virtually every interaction with their parents.*

Why These Two? (page 47)

In parenting literature throughout the ages, grace and truth stand out. Mostly, one hears them referred to as love and limits. Why? Because back in the beginning God created human beings in his own image.

- Again and again the Bible describes God as a God of grace and truth, of compassion and truth, of mercy and righteousness.

  — When have you experienced God's grace, compassion, or mercy in a very personal way? Be specific. Did his grace seem completely divorced from his truth in those circumstances? Explain.

  — When have you experienced God's truth and righteousness in a very personal way? Again, be specific. Did God's truth seem completely divorced from his grace in that situation? Explain.

— King David prayed, "Do not withhold your mercy from me, O LORD; may your love and your truth always protect me" (Psalm 40:11). Why does love offer some protection? Why does truth offer protection? Why do the two in concert offer even greater protection?

• As God lives out his grace and truth, we are to live them out as well. We need to have the love that sustains our relationships and the truth that guides us to safety and good performance—but we are not born with these qualities fully developed. Good parents help children grow and expand their capacities for grace and truth. The model of grace and truth that good parents offer their children helps the children internalize grace and truth.

— What, if anything, about your parents' modeling helped you both experience and internalize grace and truth? What can you learn about parenting from what your parents taught you by their modeling, good or bad?

— Remember Kelly's "Stupid girl. Stupid girl" when she dropped the doll (page 49)? That response was quite different from the four-year-old who exclaimed, "Oops! That's okay!" as she went to get some paper towels to clean up the Coke she had just spilled. What, if anything at this point, has your child's behavior suggested about the kind of voice he is internalizing, one of truth without grace or one of grace? If you haven't noticed anything yet, take a few moments to consider what you may be modeling—because you're being watched very carefully!

- The maxim is this: "What was once outside becomes inside." Give children grace and give them truth. But don't give one without the other. Children will not be able to put grace and truth together if they have not experienced them together. Let children discover that reality—the truth—is actually *for* them and not *against* them.

  — When was the first time you realized for yourself that reality, or truth, is actually for you? Describe the situation, what prompted your insight, and your reaction to it.

  — What does your experience suggest to you about what you can do as a parent to help your children see that reality or truth is for them, not against them? You might teach your child, for instance, that if he shows restraint and doesn't whine to have cookies at the store, he avoids losing the toy he brought along in the car during the ride home. Give one or two other possible scenarios from your own home.

Grace shows children favor, that someone is for them and on their team. It helps them tolerate dealing with the truth. Truth shows them that reality is real and how to live it. Give children both—as well as the important ingredient we'll look at in the next chapter.

Hands-on Exercise

If You Do One Thing Besides Pray . . .

We express grace when we show empathy; we express truth when we explain what limits are necessary in a given situation. List three recent conflicts with your toddler or preschooler.

1.

2.

3.

Grace: For each, note what your child might have been feeling (tired, frustrated, angry, and so on). With what words could you speak to such feelings?

Truth: What limits do you need to set in each situation you described? With what words could you clearly set and stick by those limits?

Folded-Hands Exercise

"My help comes from the LORD . . ."

—PSALM 121:2

Father God, I can't give to my child what I don't have myself. Please show me which way I tend to err—toward grace or truth—and then, Spirit, work in my heart to teach me and transform me. Help me integrate grace and truth where I haven't, so that I can give to my children a taste of the parent love—with its perfect balance of grace and truth—that you give me. I pray in Jesus' name. Amen.

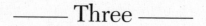

—— Three ——

The Ingredient of Time

Parents can learn a lot from Kayo Dottley. That football coach gave his players the grace of his encouragement and the truth of his knowledge and correction, and he mixed those with the needed time to build the skills and character they would need for later success. Let's take a look at some of the ways the ingredient of time works for a growing child.

The Nature and Importance of Time (page 51)

In this chapter we want to look at time and its relation to a child's development. We will consider the time you need to put in, how you structure that time, and the amounts and kinds of time the child needs.

- Look back at your own childhood and the time you spent with your parents.

  — How much time did your mother or father invest in raising you? Refer to three or four scenes from your childhood to support your sense that it was a lot of time or a little or something in between.

— How did your parents structure their time with you? Again, refer to a few specific moments from your childhood.

— Did the time your parents gave you meet your needs? Explain your answer.

- Now consider the time you are spending with each of your children.

 — How much time in a typical day and a typical week are you intentionally investing in them? "Intentionally investing" means focusing on the child's growth, not simply watching television together or running errands with him tagging along. It might mean, for instance, time spent playing, reading, or teaching a skill.

 — Describe the structure you give your time with your child.

 — Are you giving enough time to meet his needs? On what are you basing your answer?

Let's look at how the three aspects of time listed above—the time you need to put in, how you structure that time, and the amounts and kinds of time the child needs—relate to your child.

More Time, Please (page 52)

The story of Kayo shows the importance of quantities of time. With all of the time he gave, his players were able to develop the skills they needed.

- "Quality time" versus "quantity time" is a false choice society often presents parents. Why is quality time alone insufficient for a child's development?

Quantity of time is important because growth is happening—continuously—and you must be there throughout the process.

- Quantity of time is also important because children internalize things from the outside world as they grow, so you have to be constantly monitoring what they internalize. The analogy here is filling a car's tank with gas. A child takes in love and structure and converts them into character. Just as an engine can't suck down all twenty gallons at once and get you to the destination instantly, you can't feed love and structure into your child all at once. You need to distribute the fuel as the child needs it.

— What about the car engine analogy do you find helpful?

— As your child's world widens (baby-sitters, preschool, Sunday school, friends, friends' older siblings, etc.), what influences do you expect you will have to address and even correct?

— Consider your child's journey toward adolescence and adulthood. What kind of regular fuel stops do you want to schedule? At what points might there be an intense need for refueling, for feeding love and structure into your child? Transition periods such as moving, the birth of a sibling, meeting the new baby-sitter, or entering preschool are some possibilities.

- Quantity of time is important because children need to grow in relationship with another person in order to develop character. We can only truly mature in relationship with other people because relationship provides safety, love, encouragement, truth, and reality. For some people, various aspects of their personalities have been developed outside of relationship and have never been accepted or affirmed by another person. These aspects of the child (assertiveness, pain, or sexuality, for instance) remain hidden in a dark corner of the soul.

  — Imagine a little girl growing up with parents who withdraw every time she asserts herself. While other aspects of the child (such as her love and compliance) are in relationship, her parents' withdrawal means that her separateness is in isolation. Their daughter may grow up to be a woman who can't set limits because there was no love to nurture her assertiveness, or she might become a woman who can set limits but, based on her early experience, feels alone and guilty when she does. What aspect(s) of your personality were not accepted or affirmed by another person as you were growing up?

  — Look again at Debbie's story (page 54 in the text). What, if anything, does it show you about yourself? What does it show you about the kind of parenting you do or do not want to do?

— Your child needs to experience all of the aspects of himself with you. He needs to bring the following aspects of himself into relational experience with you over time. Which of these aspects might you be uncomfortable embracing, and why? What can you do to overcome that hesitation rather than communicate it to your child?

Needs	Failure
Weakness	Talents
Vulnerability	Opinions
Hurt	Assertiveness
Sadness	Honesty
Anger	Sexuality
Strength	

When you spend time with all aspects of your children, they are able to integrate all of those aspects of themselves into relationship and not have hidden, split-off parts to their character. Those experiences take quantities of time, but make sure that you are not just passing time and that instead you are relating to all the different aspects of your child.

The Way the Process Works (page 55)

Teaching and internalizing character requires a certain kind of experience of time, not just "knowledge." Internalizing a new skill, habit, or moral teaching is a process—one that involves ignorance, failure, and disobedience on the part of the child and discipline, encouragement, and teaching on the part of the parent.

- Review the five steps in the process of teaching and internalizing character outlined on pages 56–57 of the text and highlighted below. Then apply the process to two current parenting issues with your toddler or preschooler (such as not hitting, staying at the table during a meal, saying "please," or putting toys away).

  1. Introduce children to the reality. Don't expect your children to know what you expect.
  2. Allow children to experience the limits of their abilities. Children will fail when they try something new, but a parent must set a limit by saying

that to disobey a rule is "not okay" if inherent rebellion is behind the "failure."

3. Transform the failure. When failure and discipline hurt, empathize with and contain your child's feelings. Empathy paves the way for children to identify with the limit or reality of their performance. In contrast, anger, guilt, and shame distance them from the reality they need to internalize.

4. Help the child to identify with the reality. If children feel understood and loved while they see the reality of their actions (#3), they will take in the reality of the rule. It becomes part of them.

5. Encourage your child to try again. When learning new skills, children have to try and fail and then try again.

Situation #1	**Situation #2**
1.	1.
2.	2.
3.	3.
4.	4.
5.	5.

- Character development requires experience. You cannot tell children how to do something and instantly expect them to do it correctly. Instead, you must walk them through the process, help them when they fail, and aid them in making normal failure a learning experience that becomes part of their character.

— What did you learn about failure as you were growing up?

— What might you do to help your child make normal failure a learning experience?

The learning steps are a specific sequence of events in time. This is why parenting takes time and cannot be done from a distance. The child needs time to go through the experience, and the parent needs time to discipline and to empathize with the child's failure. Then the experience becomes character.

The Time the Child Needs (page 58)

Most parents realize that they have to spend time with their children. Let's look at why time is important for the child.

- Children cannot accomplish certain tasks before they're developmentally (neurologically, physically) ready.

— In what area of life or toward what behavioral goal might you be pushing your toddler or preschooler too much?

— Review the normal timeline for a child's development (pages 59–60) and some of the tasks appropriate to different stages of development (pages 61–62), focusing especially on where a child the age of yours typically is. What did you learn about your child?

 — What, if anything, did you see about where to stop pushing your child?

 — In what areas of life, if any, could you be encouraging your child to move ahead?

• One reason parents should not expect too much too soon is that there are critical windows of time for certain developmental tasks. The general thinking is that children need to go through these stages at the appropriate time because windows open up at a certain time in a child's development. For example, requiring absolute obedience from a child less than a year old disrupts the more important task a child is working on at that age. During this time the most important tasks are learning to trust, take in love, and stabilize the entire emotional and neurobiological system.

— As a child, were you ever pushed to learn a certain skill before (you now realize) you were developmentally ready? What were the results of being pushed? What, if anything, have you needed to try to "make up later"?

— In what ways is our culture rushing your child to grow up? What can you do to stand strong against that pervasive pressure?

As Solomon said, "There is a time for everything, and a season for every activity under heaven" (Ecclesiastes 3:1). So don't rush your child; enjoy the process of growing up and maturing.

Remember All Three (page 63)

We have talked about the time you must put in, the way this time gets structured, and the time a child needs. We feel strongly that time is a necessary ingredient for growth.

- Time, however, must be integrated with the other two important ingredients we've addressed—grace and truth. Here's the formula:

Grace + Truth over Time = Growth

— Why is giving grace and truth from time to time insufficient?

— Why is giving only truth over time prison?

— Why is giving only grace over time disastrous?

Your children need to know that you are on their side, and that is grace. They need to know that you will give them reality, and that is truth. And they need it pretty much every day, from birth to their late teens. Take a deep breath—and have a good time!

Now that you know the three ingredients you need to raise a great kid, we will describe how you can go about using these three ingredients in developing the six character traits every child needs to become a mature adult.

Hands-on Exercise

If You Do One Thing Besides Pray . . .

What plan will you make for regularly spending time with your child? Of course, what you do together will change as your child grows, but it's not too early to start enjoying one-on-one time with your child. So when will you go out for ice cream or visit the local park? Is every Saturday a good starting point for investing time in your child and fueling her tank with love and limits?

Folded-Hands Exercise

"My help comes from the LORD . . ."

—PSALM 121:2

Father God, you've given me many gifts—your Son, forgiveness, the hope of eternal life with you, a family, a home, finances, food, clothes. You've also given the gift of time. Lord, I confess poor stewardship in that area and my tendency to let the sin of busyness rather than godly priorities guide my use of time. Lord, you have also given me charge over my children. Teach me to live so that my daily planner reflects my commitment to them. Help me stand strong against the culture that says quality time is adequate. May I spend quantity time with them that is also quality time in which I point my children to you. I pray in Jesus' name and for his—and my children's—sake. Amen.

Part Two

Developing the Six Character Traits
Every Child Needs

Four

Laying the Foundation of Life
Connectedness

- Connectedness is the capacity to relate to God and others on a deeply personal level.
- Connectedness begins at birth and is foundational to all growth and morality.
- The development of connectedness in children requires specific tasks on the part of both parent and child.

Remember Chris? He was comfortable in his own world, which had lots of good things in it, but no people. And he wasn't lonely. There was simply no connectedness with other people, and that problem with connectedness probably started in the first three years of his life.

Life Equals Relationship (page 68)

Because Chris was unable to make attachments, he was separated from life itself. He didn't experience a need for connection, but he was suffering from this lack of connection.

- Attachment, which may seem oddly categorized as a "character trait," is foundational to all morality and is the most important trait you'll address in this book. Attachment is the capacity to relate to God and others, to connect to something outside of ourselves. When we make an attachment, good things—such as empathy, comfort, truth, and encouragement—are transferred between us and others. Attachment brings warmth, meaning, and purpose to life.

  — What evidence have you seen in your child that, from the womb, children are designed to connect?

— Why is attachment "foundational to all morality"?

Attachment is not humanity's idea, but God's. God himself is relational at his core: He is love (1 John 4:8). In some fashion that we don't fully understand, the Father, Son, and Spirit are connected and related to each other at all times. God is always in relationship with the persons of the Trinity.

The Importance of Attachment (page 69)

We cannot overemphasize the importance of developing your child's ability to attach. All of the tasks of life are based, at some level, on how connected we are to God and others. You cannot lose by developing your child's ability to re-late, because the attached child is never left without a way to get the resources necessary for life.

- Life brings many demands, problems, and requirements. Connected children look within themselves for what they can provide and then go to God and others for the rest. Detached children fend for themselves, being unable to reach out for resources and help.

  — Would you describe yourself as a connected or a detached child? Support your answer with specific details.

  — What contributed to your being connected or detached? Learn from what your parents did or didn't do. Did they, for instance, comfort you when you were sad or afraid, or were they distant when you needed reassurance?

  — Why does it make sense that kids who are emotionally connected in healthy ways are more secure and better able to delay gratification, respond to discipline, deal with failure, and make good moral decisions? (The list does go on and on.)

Dylan and Spencer were very different kids and therefore took very different approaches to a similar problem. Dylan knew he couldn't deal with the problem himself, so he went to his parents and received comfort, support, and structure so that together they could solve the problem. Spencer, however, wasn't able to reach out to family and friends to meet life's demands.

Infancy: The Birthplace of Attachment (0–12 Months) (page 71)

- Research supports the biblical idea that relationship is crucial to life. Severe disruption of the attachment between mother and child in the early months of life can affect the child's entire life.

  — In your own words, explain how important your own attachment to your baby is to his or her growth and development.

  — What are you doing to establish this early connection with your child? How might it be disrupted?

Children who are allowed to emotionally depend on reliable, loving parents become fortified with the assurance of their stability. As children internalize their mother's love, they feel safe enough to confidently explore the world.

Attachment Goals for Your Child (page 72)

The ability to connect can be broken down into different categories. Let's look at each one.

- **Use Relationship for Equilibrium:** Good attachment stabilizes children. Just as God quiets his people with his love (Zephaniah 3:17), you can quiet your child's turmoil with your attachment.

   — Do you think your toddler or preschooler finds you interested and involved in his life? safe enough? predictable enough? On what do you base your answer?

   — What are you doing to continue being bonded to your growing youngster?

   — What way(s) of showing your love does your child respond to most enthusiastically?

- **Learn Basic Trust and Need:** Basic trust is your child's ability to see the world of relationships as having enough goodness for her. You can help foster basic trust by being a "good-enough" parent—that is, being responsive at the right times and in the right ways without being perfect, just a lot more good than bad.

   — Is your own basic trust (as defined above) solid and unshakable? If so, why? If not, why not? Learn from your answers a lesson to apply to your parenting.

— Describe what a "good-enough" parent would do in one or two frequent parenting situations you face: a three-year-old who is chattering non-stop; the day's third spilled glass of milk; failure to share a toy; grabbing something from another child; a preschooler interrupting rather than waiting a turn; a toddler wanting you to read the current favorite book for the fourth time in a row.

- **Value Relationships:** One aspect of maturity is being able to value and appreciate others' love and sacrifice for us. This creates in children important traits like a heart of gratitude for others and the ability to seek out and connect to people who treat them right.

 — You can help your child become a people-oriented person by talking to her and listening to her. In general, on a scale of 1 to 10 (1 being "totally preoccupied with something else" and 10 being "totally focused on your child"), how well do you listen to your child? What does your answer show you about yourself?

 — Now consider how you talk to your child. Is it interactive? Are you both talking and listening? Is your child learning from conversations with you to both talk and listen?

 — What are you (or could you be) doing to teach your toddler or preschooler that her actions affect you and sometimes even hurt you?

— What are you doing to teach and require heartfelt gratitude?

- *Internalize Love:* Your child's many experiences of safety and consistency combine over time into a stable internal mental and emotional representation of you. Ultimately, a child doesn't think, "Mom loves me, so I'm okay," but "I'm a loved person, and I'm okay."

  — Are you being there for your child—for the fun stuff (reading books and playing ball) as well as the necessary "life" stuff (feeding, bathing, getting dressed)—in quantity as well as quality? Point to specific examples.

— Going to sleep in their own beds, learning to feed themselves, and staying in the care of baby-sitters all help children become more independent. What steps like these are you regularly allowing your child to take? Give specific examples.

- *Develop Capacity for Loss:* Success in life involves learning to deal with loss. A connected child learns to protest, mourn, and resolve loss by bringing loss to relationship and eventually letting go. Children who don't attach may devalue what they lose, stay stuck in a protest mode, or chronically mourn.

  — How does your child typically deal with loss?

— With what kinds of words do you sympathize with your child's loss (the fact that she's not getting what she wants when she wants it, for instance)? (Don't change your mind and alter the limits so that your child can avoid sadness! The lesson that such action teaches isn't helpful!)

- **Develop Gender Roles:** As kids grow into the preschool years, they begin learning how to attach to same sex and different sex people in distinctive ways. Little boys want both to be like and to compete with Dad; little girls do the same with Mom. Girls want to marry their dad and boys, their mom. Parents need to contain and structure these intense feelings for their kids.

  — What evidence have you seen that your preschool child is wanting both to be like and to compete with the same-sex parent?

  — What are you saying to contain and structure the expression of those feelings?

- **Relate to the World:** Children use relationship as a springboard of safety from which to explore the world of preschool, games, imagination, sports, and peers. Attachment helps children sort through what they like and don't like.

  — What aspects of the world is your child currently exploring? What are you doing to encourage that exploration?

— What is your child liking and not liking these days? What are you doing to further develop her interests in sports, art, music, or a specific skill? What might you do to broaden her horizons?

- ***Develop Give-and-Take:*** Another aspect of growing up is learning that relationships require give-and-take.

   — The ability to understand give-and-take develops during the early school years. What evidence do you see in your child that he isn't there yet, that he sees connections with people in terms of his own interests?

  — What are you modeling about give-and-take in the relationships your child witnesses you in?

- ***Teach Altruism:*** The most mature attachment skill is selfless giving. Altruism is giving out of concern for another without regard to oneself. It is the essence of God's love.

   — Growing up is a pretty self-centered endeavor, but kids can nevertheless learn all the way through life that they can comfort with the comfort that they themselves have received (2 Corinthians 1:3–4). What opportunities to begin to teach altruism to your toddler or preschooler do you find in your family? in play groups? in church settings?

— What selfless love (*not* martyr love, but a love based on free and good-natured choice) are you showing to your child? Consider times you've expressed empathy or gratitude. When, if ever, have you been able to reward your child for showing compassion for friends?

Again, while the foundational "inviting to life" work is done in the first year, helping children with bonding experiences continues throughout their childhood.

How Attachment Happens (page 77)

Specific tasks create the ability to connect. Children have their job: they must experience the reality that relationship is good and that it brings the necessary elements of life. Mothers (or the primary caregiver) have their job: they invite their children into relationship by responding to their children and meeting their needs. These two jobs interact to help children become capable of making attachments to people.

• Think back on your own childhood and how this dance played itself out.

— In the home in which you grew up, did you experience the reality that relationship is good, that it brings the necessary elements of life? If not, when and from whom did you learn those essential lessons? If you still need to learn these lessons, what might you do to reach that goal? Our books *Changes That Heal* (Henry Cloud, Zondervan, 1992) and *Hiding from Love* (John Townsend, Zondervan, 1996) can help.

— What did your mother do to invite you into relationship? In what ways did she respond to you? In what manner did she meet your needs?

Let's now look more closely at the tasks involved for both the child and the mother.

- ### *The Child's Tasks:*

  — *Experience, and respond to, the need for relationship.* How does your young child express his relational needs (for comfort, encouragement, love, affection) and functional needs (for food, a clean diaper, help with a toy)? What are his most effective ways of getting your attention?

  — *Keep signaling the need.* Infants have very little capacity to tolerate being in need for long periods of time. How can you encourage your child to keep trying to let you know that she needs something so that she doesn't give up too soon?

  — *Receive the good.* What evidence have you seen that children don't receive the good passively, that instead they go out to find it and then actively respond to love? Why is this trait helpful for children who, by virtue of their youth, have lots of empty places inside them that need to be filled with love?

As children perform the three tasks just outlined, they receive the fuel for existence and experience the goodness of relationship, so that they continue to seek relationships.

- ### *The Parent's Tasks:*

  — *Respond to the need.* What support do you have as you tackle the (especially in the early stages) exhausting and taxing work of meeting your child's needs?

— Children need predictability. What structure and consistency (such as responding appropriately and in a timely fashion) have you gradually built—or are you gradually building—into your child's world?

— How do you respond to the argument that an infant's expression of his needs is his sinful attempt to control and dominate the family? What is the child really trying to communicate?

 — Ideally, in their first twelve months, children learn that the world is a reasonably safe place, and then they are ready to move on and explore the world. If your child is one year or older, what are you doing (or could you start doing) to help your child with these qualities:

Delay of gratification

Patience

Learning to self-soothe when you are absent

Appropriate discipline

— *Respond appropriately*. The younger the children, the less able they are to tell you the nature of their need. What cues have you come to recognize in your child?

— *Present relational solutions to relational needs*. Whether your child needs connection for her isolation, hurt, or loneliness or needs answers, suggestions, advice, and problem solving for her functional needs, what do you do (or could you do) to teach her that relationship comes before anything? By what words and actions do you try to show understanding, warmth, and empathy? How do you show your child that you are listening to her? Do you, for example, let her finish her sentence before you respond? Do you help draw out her feelings so that she learns that feelings are okay? Do you stay connected to her when she protests? Do you make sure you understand your child's emotions before you address or try to contain them?

— When has simply connecting solved what appeared to be a functional problem? That happens occasionally.

— Sticking a bottle in a lonely infant's mouth is an example of attempting to solve relational problems functionally. Evaluate your tendency to solve relational problems functionally. Is that tendency a problem for you? If so, under what circumstances are you most likely to do so?

— *Connect without intrusiveness.* When have you seen your child suddenly move on from needing closeness to needing freedom? What is a wise way for parents to move from their children's need for closeness to their children's need for freedom?

— Do you experience relationship as controlling or enmeshing and closeness as something that will destroy, violate, or imprison you? If so, think back on how your parents may have been intrusive when you were a child. What can you learn from your own childhood and apply to your own parenting?

— The Bible says that genuine love is not self-seeking (1 Corinthians 13:5). Why is this truth good for parents to remember, especially when it comes to connecting to one's child without being intrusive?

Parent your children to experience connectedness and to be able to safely receive and give love. Teaching children this kind of connectedness helps build inside them a connected foundation that will sustain them for life. This connected foundation is also the necessary building block for the aspect of character we'll be discussing in the next chapter: learning responsibility.

Hands-on Exercise

If You Do One Thing Besides Pray . . .

Often we can think we're communicating love to someone, adult or child. But what we're doing or saying may not feel like love to the recipient. What words or actions most clearly communicate love to your child? If you're not sure, become a student of your child. Do gifts, time, hugs, words, notes, or something else make your child feel most loved? If you know what makes your child feel loved, consider how often you speak that language of love to him or her—and start making it a habit if it isn't already.

Folded-Hands Exercise

"My help comes from the LORD . . ."

—PSALM 121:2

Almighty God, this chapter has reminded me in no uncertain terms how important this task of parenting is, and it's easy to feel overwhelmed. Thank you that my help does come from you. Please help me, Lord, to know how to use relationship with my children for their growth and equilibrium. Guide me as I try to teach them to trust that relationship is good; to come to value relationships; to help them internalize love; to develop a capacity for loss; to develop healthy gender roles; to relate to the world; to learn give-and-take; and to learn altruism. Give me wisdom as I tackle my tasks as a parent. Teach me to respond to my children's needs—and to respond appropriately; to present relational solutions to relational needs; and to connect without being intrusive.

May I lean on you day by day, moment by moment, trusting you to make me a "good-enough" parent. And use me in my children's lives so that they will be able to attach to you, their heavenly Father. I pray in Jesus' name. Amen.

—— Five ——

Developing Self-Control
Responsibility

┌─ **Parenting Principles** ─────────────────────

- Responsibility is the capacity to own one's life as one's problem.
- Self-control and learning limits are necessary for responsibly choosing the good and refusing the bad.
- The four qualities involved in teaching kids responsibility are love, truth, freedom, and reality.

└───

The task of parenting is to transform the child's stance from "My life is my parents' problem" to "Yikes, my life is my problem! Though my parents love me, they aren't going to clean up all the messes I make in life." And this is the second great aspect of character: the capacity to take responsibility for one's life.

Responsibility Puts Love into Action (page 87)

Caring parents want their children to do well in life. "Doing well" has to do with the functional aspects of living, how one performs. The key to "doing well" is responsibility.

- We define responsibility as *the capacity to own one's life as one's problem.* It is the parent's job to help structure their children's time and energy into activities that develop responsibility.

  — How well did you learn to be responsible as you were growing up? More specifically, what evidence of your responsibility (or irresponsibility) can you point to in your life?

73

— How were those lessons about responsibility (positive or negative) taught to you? Give an example or two. Were you, for example, consistently rewarded for good behavior and consistently disciplined for bad?

- Choices (between good and bad) and information (about the dangers of the bad) are indeed important to a child's decision making, but children need to practice self-control, delay of gratification, and setting and receiving limits before they can responsibly choose the good and refuse the bad.

  — Think back over your life. When have you chosen the bad because you didn't practice self-control, couldn't delay gratification, or didn't set limits or acknowledge the limits that were set for you?

  — When has the practice of self-control, the delay of gratification, or the setting or honoring of limits enabled you to choose the good?

 — In what small ways can you give your toddler or preschooler some practice in self-control? delaying gratification? honoring limits you set? Could you, for instance, set limits and establish consequences for tantrums rather than nagging, pleading, or threatening?

- The primary function of responsibility is to put love into action, to develop love by performing good works that God foreordained for us (Ephesians 2:10). *Relationship is the reason for existence. Responsibility is the means of bringing about and protecting relationship.*

— What role does responsibility have in keeping alive your love for your spouse or a close friend?

— Attachment and responsibility were designed to grow together in your child in the same way that love and truth are to be integrated in your parenting. Have you ever met any nice but irresponsible children? In each case, who was paying for the children's lack of control or ownership of their life?

Nice kids can be irresponsible kids. Love and limits must go together. When they do, the fruit is great. If you have any doubt, look again at page 89 and the list of abilities that comes with learning to be responsible.

Develop Responsibility With or Without Your Child's Permission (page 90)

Having a child who takes responsibility for her life is a good and appropriate dream for parents. Yet there is one fundamental problem: from the beginning, the child has no interest whatsoever in becoming responsible.

• Children can't see value in taking responsibility for a problem.

— What evidence of this truth, if any, have you seen in your young child?

— What do parents teach their children if they often take on responsibilities for their children that the kids should be bearing for themselves? When, for instance, have you noticed that, once you stop requiring your child to pick up her toys, she begins expecting you to, having concluded that it is no longer her job, but yours?

— What lessons about responsibility, and what truths or untruths about yourself and your abilities, did you learn from the way your parents did or didn't take on that which was your responsibility?

- ***Boundaries: Bringing Responsibility to Your Child's Experience:*** Setting boundaries for your children is a central part of developing responsible character in them. Boundaries are a person's property line. They point out where you end and others begin. They allow you to know what belongs to you and what belongs to another. They allow you to know what you are and are not responsible for.

— Parents appropriately structure their children's lives so that they are free to make choices that will either reward them for responsibility or cause them pain for irresponsibility. Children experience and internalize these boundaries for themselves. What small consequences have you set (or could you set) for your children that reward them for responsibility? Could you, for example, give your child a hug for being kind to a sibling?

— What boundaries have you set (or could you set) for your children that cause them pain for irresponsibility? Could you enforce a clean-up routine with the consequence of losing a toy for a certain length of time?

- ***The Parent's Task: Love, Truth, Freedom, and Reality:*** As the interaction between Kevin and Allison illustrated, children are not your ally in your efforts to teach them responsibility. In their minds, they have much to lose and nothing to gain by taking responsibility for their life. But the good news is that they are going to resist responsibility whether you handle it rightly or wrongly.

— Comment on Allison's change from frustrated psycho-mom to the calm parent who enforced logical consequences for Kevin's failure to take responsibility for his toys. What do you like about her second approach?

— To what situation(s) in your home can you apply lessons you learned from this scene with Allison?

- The responsibility you need to teach your children can be broken down into four qualities: love, truth, freedom, and reality. As you provide these qualities in the right sequences, types, and amounts, you set up a structure for your children that makes irresponsibility painful and responsibility pleasurable. And children grow as responsibility becomes internalized and part of their character structure.

— ***Love:*** What do you do (or could you do) to show your children that, even when you and they disagree, you are "for" them—concerned about their welfare, safety, best interests, and growth? How, for example, do you reassure them of your love during the conflict rather than withdrawing emotionally? What do you say to stay focused on the issue or behavior instead of attacking your children when you disagree?

— Think about the relationship between love and law you experienced as you were growing up. Did your parents' love give you the freedom to protest the rules of the household as you were learning to abide by those rules? Give an example. Did your parents' love free you from self-judgment when you failed? Again, give an example.

Invest time and energy in cementing your love for your children and offering them clear statements of grace. Keep in mind, too, that kids tend to shoot the messenger carrying the responsibility lesson. It hurts for a child to hate you, but that is part of the burden of being a parent.

— **Truth:** It's hard to hold someone accountable for misbehaving when that person hasn't been told the truth. What do you do to make sure your children understand the boundaries you are setting for them?

— Look again at the Truth column of the table in chapter 2 of the text (pages 43–45) and review what your children can handle at their age. What chores can become partly your child's responsibility if they aren't already?

— Consider how you present truths to your child. Even at this stage, what few universal rules might replace many specific rules? What truths are you currently praying about, asking God to guide you as you determine how to present them to your children? What trusted people can you turn to for counsel about your presentation of truths? What will you do to memorialize the rules for your not-yet-reading child?

— **Freedom:** Freedom allows children to experience their choices—and the consequences of those choices—for themselves. When you were growing up, did you have the freedom to disobey? What did that freedom (or its absence) teach you? How did freedom foster the growth of responsibility or the lack of freedom inhibit it? Were you given consequences when you exercised that freedom in bad ways?

— Think about your interactions with your child. Could he be living in fear of loss of love, abandonment, attack, or condemnation if he rejects your rules? Explain why you answered as you did.

— You could undoubtedly identify with the green-bean situation. What parenting moments remind you that you can't control your child? Choose two or three of those situations and, away from the heat of the moment, develop right reasons for getting your child to do what you want her to do. The consequence of no dessert until the beans are eaten is a right reason or logical consequence for not eating the vegetables she put on her plate. Not seeing a favorite TV show or spending some time away from family fun can also be a right reason for behaving.

— **Reality:** Parenting needs to mirror the real world as much as possible, and in the real world adults experience painful consequences for their irresponsibility. When have consequences taught you an important lesson about responsibility? Ideally refer to a childhood experience.

— Review the list of qualities that make consequences effective (pages 101–2), and then look at consequences you've established through the lens those qualities provide. Are the consequences you've used—

As close to natural consequences as possible?
Appropriate to the child's developmental maturity level?
Appropriately severe?
Administered ASAP?
Loving?
As specific as possible?
Flexible?

— Keeping in mind those seven characteristics of effective consequences, establish some consequences for common infractions in your home.

These four responsibility builders—love, truth, freedom, and reality—all work together to create a learning and internalizing environment for children. Generally, as parents remain consistent with these four, children will protest, test, and escalate for a while. When the children see that you are serious and that you are stronger than they, they will develop the limits for themselves.

The Fruits of Responsibility (page 102)

Whatever their age, you can expect, observe, and encourage some things in your children as character develops, as they begin "getting it."

- **Ownership:** Children begin to look less to you and more to themselves to take care of their problems.

  — What signs have you seen in your preschooler that he is beginning to be an effective steward of his behavior, attitudes, emotions, and relationships?

  — What are you modeling in the way of stewardship over one's behavior, attitudes, emotions, and relationships?

- **Self-control:** As children experience consistent, appropriate consequences, they take in the structure.

— What evidence, if any, have you seen that a structure of appropriate consequences helps your younger preschooler work through temper tantrums or your older preschooler practice concentrating? Holding off playtime until chores are done, using an egg timer to structure clean-up time, and following up when you warn your child that you will discipline him could be effective consequences.

— When have you caught (or later heard about) your child doing a good thing when you weren't looking over her shoulder and coaching her? What did you tell her in response to learning that news?

• **Freedom:** As children develop self-control, they create the space in their heads to think maturely about their choices. Self-control helps them take stock of what they should and shouldn't do.

— When has your child seemed to stop and consider a choice he was about to make? Be specific.

— What did his choice reveal about your child and, specifically, about his progress toward being a responsible individual?

While you are training your children in responsibility, don't wait for them to rise up and call you blessed. But do be encouraged by those moments when you see them developing ownership and self-control and then using that self-control to freely make good, value-based decisions.

The Motive Issue (page 104)

Parents want their children to grow up to be responsible and faithful because they care and want to do the right thing, not because they're afraid of the consequences of doing the wrong thing.

- Motives are developmental: children start life as lawless and self-centered individuals and probably develop more "pure" motives to do right as they grow older. Altruism and love of God are the highest motives, but none of us is mature enough to be driven only by these.

— What encouragement do you find in these truths about motives?

— Describe a time early on when you did the right thing because you knew it was right rather than because you feared the consequences. How old were you? What conversation went on in your head? Do you still have those conversations? What helps you today to choose to do the good and right, to act out of love for God, or to serve others? What does your own experience suggest about how you as a parent can start addressing the motive issue with your young child?

Accept the fact that you and your child are alike: you both love and care, but you both have a wayward part that needs to know about reality.

Attachment and responsibility form so much of a child's character. Next we will deal with how to help children solve a problem as old as humankind: dealing with the reality of imperfection.

Hands-on Exercise

If You Do One Thing Besides Pray . . .

The next time you need to reinforce the importance of following rules or truth, a tangible fence or boundary might help. Take your child to a local fenced-in playground, ideally next to a busy street. Talk about how easy and safe it would be to play ball since the fence surrounds the play area. Then get your child thinking about what it would be like to try to play on the playground if the fence were gone. Help your child conclude that fences (boundaries) mean safety and protection. Explain as simply as possible that your rules do the same job that fence does: give your child safety and protection.

Folded-Hands Exercise

"My help comes from the LORD . . ."

—PSALM 121:2

Lord God, what an encouragement to realize that self-control is a fruit of your Holy Spirit's work in our lives! And what a call to pray for my child—and for myself as I do my part to prepare the way for the Spirit to do his work in my child's heart. And, Lord, I do pray for myself that you would give me strength to persist when my child doesn't like his training in responsibility; creativity and insight as I establish boundaries and then the courage to enforce them; and wisdom and guidance as I try to balance love, truth, freedom, and reality in my efforts to raise my child to be responsible. May I rely on you with each step I take on this important path! In Jesus' name. Amen.

Six

Living in an Imperfect World
Reality

Parenting Principles

- Losing well is one of the most important character traits parents can develop in their children.
- Kids need help dealing with imperfection in themselves, other people, and the world.
- For a child, being loved should become more central than being good enough.

We don't like to lose. But in reality, we all do. And what ultimately separates the winners from the losers is not that winners lose less. It is that they lose better. And losing well, with the ability to continue on, is one of the most important character traits you can develop in your child.

The Lost Ideal (page 107)

Reality is a place where things do not always go as we would like. When we fail, or circumstances or relationships do not turn out as we had hoped, we have to keep going and try to make the best of a bad situation. Your children's ability to do this will determine how well their lives go.

- What do you like about how you handle loss? What would you like to be able to do better when loss comes your way?

- Review the list of some ways children experience "lost ideals" on page 107 of the text. Which of the first four behaviors listed have you seen in your child?

As a friend of mine says to her young son, "Livin's hard." Your job is to make the hard job of living no more difficult than it has to be. You can do this by building character into your child that is able to overcome the pain and loss that everyone encounters.

The Real Loss (page 108)

In the real world, the one where we all have to live, we have a conflict between how things should be (as they were in the Garden of Eden: everything was "good") and how they really are (in our less-than-perfect world of sin and loss). As Jesus said, "In the world you have tribulation" (John 16:33 NASB).

- What losses have you experienced in your life?

- What is the earliest experience of loss you remember? What can you recall from that situation that can help you empathize with and parent your child?

Learning to accept both the good and the bad enables your children to have a firm grounding in reality and to create a life that will help them pursue what's left of Eden, without giving up along the way.

The Three Realities (page 108)

In this world of tribulation, your children—from the beginning of their lives—are going to have to learn to overcome imperfection in three spheres: self, other people, and the world.

- *Self:* The first reality your children will have to learn to face is this: *They are not ideal or perfect.* Matt never learned to accept his own imperfection. In Matt's family there was no such thing as failure, so he and his brothers never learned that they are flawed, imperfect people who will at times fail, lose, and make mistakes.

  — How did your parents respond to your failures? Were their reactions helpful? Why or why not? How, if at all, did your parents teach you that you are not perfect?

— How do you react to your failures? How easily do you accept the fact that you are flawed and imperfect, that you (like everyone else on this planet) will fail, lose, and make mistakes? What are you modeling to your children?

— From somewhere in the second year of life on, the reality that they are flawed, imperfect people who will fail, lose, and make mistakes presents itself to your children over and over again. What encounters have your children had with this fact? Give an example or two. What did you do to help them handle the situation? What would you like to do differently next time?

Your children need to know that they are not perfect.

- **Other People:** Your children also need to learn that other people are not perfect. They want others to gratify them, to never make mistakes, and certainly never to hurt them. In reality, though, they will find a whole gamut of people out there. Some are generally good and fair; others are not. What will your children do? Will they be prepared for the variety of people they will meet?

  — What have you said (and what would you like to say) to your children about the fact that other people are not perfect?

  — What can parents do to counter the risk of raising a "brat" (someone who demands that everyone be just what she wants them to be) and a "co-dependent" (someone who tolerates destructive behavior from everyone)?

Learning to live with imperfect others is an important character trait to have.

- **The World:** Not only will your children frustrate themselves and be frustrated by others, but the world will frustrate them as well.

— What frustrations has the world introduced in your young child's life— a rained-out birthday party, a pet that died, a toy that broke, or something else?

— What did you do or say to help your child cope with that loss?

Your job is to help your children develop the character that will enable them to be joyful in a world that daily gives them opportunity to be miserable. This chapter will teach you how to develop in your children the character necessary to overcome losses, failure, sin, and evil—in themselves, in others, and in the world around them.

The Problem Defined (page 111)

In short, the problem is this: God created your children to live in a perfect world, with perfect others, and to be perfect themselves. But now, in a fallen world, they have to live with both the ideals and the imperfections.

- What can parents do and say to help their children learn to accept their imperfect self and imperfect others? Maybe you can learn something from how your parents taught you—or didn't teach you!

- How can parents force their children to deal with reality, yet continue to pursue their ideals? Again, what can you learn from your parents or other parents you have seen in action?

Only the internalized character of grace and truth can help children nego-tiate life's ups and downs. And that character can only come from many expe-riences with a loving, but truthful parent who forces them to deal with reality, accept themselves and others, and continue on to pursue their ideals.

Fig Leaves for Everyone (page 112)

When something goes wrong in life, whether inside or outside of us, we tend to make sure that neither we nor anyone else knows the truth. We have many names for this strategy, and they all fulfill the purpose of keeping the pain or badness out of our own or someone else's awareness. These strategies are aptly symbolized by Adam and Eve's fig leaves.

- When have you relied on fig leaves? Give one example.

- When have you seen your child reach for a fig leaf in order to keep pain or badness out of her or someone else's awareness?

We adults have ways of hiding from reality just as our children do. Let's look at how the fig leaves operate in the parenting process and what you should avoid.

You should be aware of four barriers to building the character your child is going to need later in life: denial of the bad things, denial of the ideals, judg-ment of the bad, and lack of experience of the bad things in life.

- **Denial of the Bad:** Subtle denial of children's problems or faults is very common in many couples' day-to-day parenting. Children readily deny their own sin and problems as well.

  — We tend to have an easier time seeing other people's flaws rather than our own. When have you seen a parent deny that her child has a prob-lem (with sharing, biting, crying rather than speaking, for instance)? Why is such denial an easier path to take?

— What problems that your child faces may you be unwilling to see? (Are you in a close enough and safe enough relationship with another family so that other parents might help you see what you aren't letting yourself see?)

 — When has your child readily denied her own sin, mistake, or problem? In your own words, explain why this is not a good pattern for life.

- **Denial of the Ideals:** The other way to deal with the tension of living both in the good and the bad is to deny the ideal altogether. That can be done in a variety of harmful ways: by labeling a child ("the black sheep of the family"), using a tone of voice that says "all bad," not being involved enough with a child, and not pushing a child to perform in reasonable ways. Parents should not deny the good in either the child or the standard.

  — Through the years you have probably learned to see your behavior as a problem to be dealt with rather than seeing yourself as all bad when you fail. Closely related to this is the question "How has the process of failure and correction helped you accept that you are not perfect, that you are neither all good nor all bad?" What lessons from your own experience of failing and being corrected can you apply to your parenting?

 — What are you doing to set a solid foundation for a lifelong pattern of being involved with your children—a lifetime of maintaining high ideals for your children and requiring each one to attain those standards; of establishing performance expectations; and of expecting failure and then correcting with grace and forgiveness? Point to specific evidence from interactions with your child.

- **Judgment of the Bad:** Judgment is the condemning emotional tone with which imperfection is met. In parenting we usually see judgment as anger or as crippling guilt messages about failure, and such judgment will keep a child from facing reality.

  — What judgment, if any, did you encounter as you were growing up? What reality did it keep you from facing? What lesson for your own parenting can you learn from your experience?

  — What might indicate that certain toddlers or preschoolers are afraid that their imperfections will cost them love or incur anger? What could a parent have done to sow seeds of such fear? What can you do to avoid sowing such seeds? Consider Ephesians 4:32.

- **Lack of Experience:** Another barrier to facing reality is a lack of experience in failure.

  — When, if ever, have you seen parents not give their child an opportunity to fail? Why might they be afraid to let their child fail?

  — What opportunities to fail have you already been able to give your young child? What lesson do you think your child started to learn from these experiences?

Denial of the bad things, denial of the ideals, judgment of the bad, and lack of experience of the bad things in life are four barriers to building character. These barriers keep children from learning from their mistakes, recognizing they're not as good as they think they are, realizing that failure doesn't cost them love, acknowledging that they do not know everything or know how to do everything, and becoming whole by integrating the "good me–bad me" split inside.

The Myth of "Positive Self-Esteem" (page 116)

There is a lot of talk today about self-esteem. Parents are careful to build it in their children. People seek it for themselves. Therapists encourage it in their clients. But the whole idea of "self-esteem" is confusing for several reasons.

- First, the idea of self-esteem places the security of children at risk by basing it on their positive performance. The concept hinges on children being able to see themselves positively. Second, with self-esteem the focus is on maintaining a good view of ourselves as opposed to maintaining relationship. Happy people don't get all caught up in themselves; they focus more on tasks and loving other people. Third, the "good self" is a proud self, and a proud self does not develop the kind of humility before God and others that results in gratitude.

  — When have you seen someone—or when have you yourself been—trapped by the myth of "positive self-esteem"? In your example(s), which of the three problems with self-esteem listed above was the greatest threat?

  — Explain in your own words why a better way than seeing ourselves as *good* is seeing ourselves as *loved*. What thoughts (if any) about an adult's encouraging "Good girl!" or "Good boy!" does this discussion prompt? What words might be better?

- We are not advocating a return to "worm theology." Seeing ourselves as only dirty rotten sinners is just as unhelpful as seeing ourselves as faultless saints. We are both bearers of God's image and sinners. We are beautiful at times and not so pretty at other times. The real question is where the safety comes from that allows us to be all that we are. And the Bible's answer to that is love (1 John 4:18).

  — In what ways has God's love for you meant safety to be both sinner and saint? In what ways is God's love moving you from sinner to saint?

  — What are you doing to teach your child about God's love? What would you like to be doing?

- In speaking against "positive self-esteem," we're not saying that children should not be praised for doing well. Children were created with a need for parental approval, so praise them for a job well done. Validating their ability to do something consolidates a feeling of competency in children and helps them internalize that feeling.

  — When has justifiable praise motivated you? If you can, think of an example from your childhood.

  — What can you expect to have the opportunity to praise your child for this week? Watch for a chance to validate their ability to do something.

Do not buy into the philosophy that building positive self-esteem is the answer to all of a child's problems. Children need, most of all, to feel loved as they are and then to be encouraged to learn how to do things well. The issue of "Am

I good enough?" will become a non-issue. A "loved self" is much more secure than a "good self" any day.

The Cure: Safe Enough to Be Real (page 118)

Making children feel bad does not motivate them to do better. Nor does making them feel good guard them from all of life's pitfalls. The answer to the self-esteem problem is this: Give them a combination of grace and truth, and they will feel safe enough to be real.

- What aspect of yourself, if any, did you feel you had to hide when you were growing up? What made you feel that way? What can parents do to keep their children from feeling they need to hide a part of themselves? Specifically, what will you do in this regard?

- Children need to learn what (hopefully) their parents have already learned: they need to know that it is okay to fail, to hurt, or to be less than perfect. They need to feel secure in bringing their bad parts to relationship.

— What are you doing to teach your children that it is okay to fail and to be less than perfect? Think about the behaviors they see in you as well as the words they hear from you.

— What are you doing to teach your children that it is okay to hurt? What do they see about how you deal with hurt? What do they receive and hear from you when they are hurt?

There is no problem that the grace and guidance of loving parents cannot get children through. But if children do not feel they can be who they really are, then their problems never get solved. They just get hidden away to grow into bigger cancers.

The Process of Embracing Reality (page 119)

How do you teach children to live in an imperfect world? You start by forcing them to face reality and giving them enough grace to embrace reality and to move on. Let's take a closer look at this process.

 • **Protest:** Give an example of a time when reality hit your child. In what ways did she (quite naturally) protest that reality, be it the pain of separation, discipline, or something else?

 • **Reality Remains:** When have you let, for instance, the reality of discipline stand rather than relenting after your child's protest? Why is that the better option? Put differently, what do parents teach their children if they rush in to change painful realities?

 • **Metabolize the Reality:** What empathy (which is grace communicated and a means by which your child experiences your love) did you extend to your child in the example you just gave? How did your child respond to that empathy?

 • **Grief:** Consider again your child's response to the empathy you offered. What evidence of mourning and then of letting go did you see? Be specific.

- **Problem Solving and Resolution:** Still working with your example, what did you do to help your child learn why she failed and to encourage her to try again? If the example was in the area of performance, did your child "get back on the horse and try again"? If the example was in the area of relationship, did your child "confront, repent, forgive, and reconcile"?

Not pain, sin, failure, or anything else can stop us if we have reality, comfort, the ability to grieve, and the courage to go on. Our God is one who brings forth victory from any defeat. And if we lose well, we can be victorious, too. This is one of the best lessons your child can ever learn: There is no loss in life great enough that facing the truth with grace and having the courage to go forward cannot cure.

Some Examples (page 123)

In the various stages of childhood (infancy, toddlerhood, early childhood, adolescence), the formula of facing the truth with grace and having the courage to go forward is the same, but the content changes. Let's consider the stages of infancy and toddlerhood.

- **Infancy:** Infants are born into loss, cut off from love and truth; they have no love and security inside them. Consider that birth is a loss of the total gratification and safety of the womb. Parents are waiting outside with open, loving arms, but the infant doesn't experience their love immediately. Rather, he experiences the loss of the womb and protests it by screaming until the mother soothes him. In light of this loss, infants do not need to be given reality. It is there from day one. Limits are not for infants. Focus instead on satisfying and comforting their needs. Love them out of their distress.

  — Explain in your own words why setting limits on infants is not necessary or wise and why you cannot spoil an infant.

— What can a parent do to love an infant out of her distress? Be specific about things like feedings, diapers, and rocking chair time.

- *Toddlerhood:* Toddlers go through the process of embracing reality when they encounter the limits you set or the limits of their own abilities. They protest. You hold the limit. They move into rage and finally give in to a sadness you can comfort.

  — What limits have you set to teach your toddler that he is not in control of the universe, to help him lose the wish to be God?

  — What truths help you stand strong when your toddler rages and protests against you and the limits you hold?

- *Being Hated:* One of the most important qualities for a parent to possess is the ability to be hated. Your child will never integrate their good and bad feelings if you are uncomfortable with their anger toward you.

  — What did you do with feelings of hatred for your parents? If you shared them, how did they respond? Was their response helpful or not? Explain.

  — How do you want to respond to your child's feelings of hatred toward you when you set a limit they don't like? Remember the importance of holding firm and offering grace.

- **_The Result:_** If all goes well with this process of embracing reality (protest, reality remains, accept reality, grief, resolution), you will throughout the years build several things into your children's character that will last them a lifetime.

 — Review the list of character traits on page 127 of the text. Which traits might you need to work on so that you can indeed help pass them on to your children?

 — If your child is past the infant and baby stage, what traits do you see beginning to develop?

The character traits you just reviewed will enable your children to live a good life—not a perfect life, but a good and satisfying life. Every day, inching toward perfection and never getting there, they will enjoy the process. If that happens, you will have done a very good job of helping them live in reality.

In the next chapter we will look at some of those realities.

Hands-on Exercise

If You Do One Thing Besides Pray . . .

Key to countering the popular cultural myth of "positive self-esteem" is teaching your child about God's love—and remembering that you are modeling it in all your interactions with her. Earlier you were asked, "What are you doing to teach your child about God's love? What would you like to be doing?" This week act on one of your ideas.

In the next day or two also look carefully for an opportunity to praise your child for a job well done (such as cleaning up her room, sorting laundry, or setting the table). Remember that children were created with a need for parental approval, so when they do a job well, let them know you approve. Validating their ability to do something consolidates a feeling of competency in children and helps them internalize that feeling.

Folded-Hands Exercise

"My help comes from the LORD . . ."

—PSALM 121:2

Almighty God, your Son was very direct: "In this world you have tribulation." Yet still the hard stuff can surprise us, and we can struggle to accept reality—the reality about ourselves, about others, and about the world around us. I think of the loss I have experienced, and I don't look forward to the losses that my children will know in their life. But I realize that being able to face reality—to acknowledge and address our imperfections, our failures, our losses—is key to growth and the development of strong character.

As I help my children learn and accept that they are not perfect, may I use those opportunities to also teach them about your love. Use me, Lord God, so that the issue of "Am I good enough?" will become a nonissue for my children. May my children know that they are loved—and may I see in their lives that a "loved self" is much more secure than a "good self" any day.

Thank you that my child and I can both rest in your love that accepts us now even as your Spirit works in us to transform us and make us more like Christ—in whose name we pray. Amen.

—— Seven ——

Developing Gifts and Talents
Competence

┌─ **Parenting Principles** ──────────────────

- Developing competence and skill in certain areas helps children take their place in, and contribute to, the adult world.
- Parents need to show their kids that work is good, important, and expected.
- Parents need to help their kids develop competency areas as well as learn the disciplines of work.

└─────────────────────────────────────

Remember how ten-year-old Ryan quietly explained body design, sanding, wheel polishing, and axle positioning to several Pinewood Derby competitors, fathers as well as sons? Showing a great command of his subject, he gave examples and showed alternatives, and those who learned from him had faster cars than previous years. Now, Ryan will probably not race derby cars full-time when he grows up—but he is well on his way to taking his place in the workforce, equipped to excel.

Your Child Is a Working Child (page 129)

Even when children are young, they have to work. Work is a central aspect of our existence. God designed us not only to be in relationship and to connect, but to be productive in the world, to contribute meaningfully to others in a significant way.

- Much of the time and energy invested in living involves some work. In which of the following areas are you seeing your child begin to work? Give a few specific examples.

  — Life skills (hygiene, clothing)

— School (day care, Sunday school, preschool, kindergarten)

— Sports/physical activity

• Children who grow up competent in something are better able to function in the adult world, where expertise is a large part of life. They will have more to offer, and they will gain more satisfaction from executing their craft well.

— As a child, what kind of encouragement toward competence did you receive—or how were you discouraged or held back?

— What, if anything, did you become competent in—or begin to become competent in—as a child? How has that experience served you well— or how has its absence been something of a handicap?

Competence is the area of character growth we will be discussing in this chapter. We will tell you how you can help your children develop the capacity to be experts in some area, to perform well as craftspeople, and to contribute meaningfully through their gifts and abilities.

Competence: Entrance into the "Adult Club" (page 130)

Teaching your children competence helps them move toward adulthood. In a way, adults form an exclusive club—it's not open to all who want to join. The club has requirements for membership.

• The first requirement is to be competent in some area. Children need to have a function or service to offer to the adult club (Proverbs 22:29).

— When they are young, your children's job is simply to grow up. It is not to contribute to the betterment of grown-ups. When have you seen parents forget this basic fact?

— Preschool children can be learning that doing things well is something that brings them praise and good things (such as friends with common interests or greater opportunities). Think of some ways you can help your child see competence in drawing, throwing a ball, helping you set the table, or the like as a good thing.

- The second requirement for entrance into the adult world is to become equal and mutual with adults. Children have moms and dads to be a safety net when they fail. Grown-ups must do things for themselves without a safety net.

— In what ways are you a safety net for your child? Be specific.

— Children's need for a parent shifts from their human parents to God himself, who wants to be their only parent (Matthew 23:9). What did your parents do, if anything, to facilitate this transition in your life? What would you like to do to help your children shift their dependence from you to God their heavenly Father?

- The third requirement for adulthood is relational. Adults connect on both a bonding and a task level. Developing some skill or expertise helps your child relate in both ways to other adults.

— When has some skill or expertise helped you connect to another adult?

— When have you seen your child connect with another child on the basis of a shared interest? What indication of increased confidence or enjoyment, if any, did you see in your child during that interaction?

The ability of children to master some gift or talent is an important source of a realistic self-image and confidence. As they "own" some interest and grow in it, they are able to experience life less as a helpless, dependent infant and more as a grown-up (Proverbs 13:19 KJV).

Love and Approval Are Different (page 131)

Children should not have their love needs tied to their performance. They should be secure in their relationship with you—no strings attached. This is the essence of grace: love that one doesn't deserve.

- Depending on how your parents separated (or didn't separate) love and approval, what did you learn about hard work and love when you were growing up?

- What are you doing (or could you be doing) to keep love and approval separate for your child? In what ways are you saying, "I love you with no strings attached. However, I don't approve of how you are handling the jobs we are giving you"?

Remember, keep love and approval separate. As a parent, you need to be "for" your children no matter how good, bad, industrious, or lazy they are.

Work Is Good, Important, and Expected (page 132)

Helping children develop competency first involves helping them create a "pro-work" attitude. You need to provide an environment in which they can in-

ternalize the reality that work—both inside and outside the home—is good, important, and expected.

- What are you and/or your spouse modeling for your children about attitude, responsibility, energy, and enthusiasm as one or both of you head off to work?

- What are you and your spouse modeling for your children about attitude, responsibility, energy, and enthusiasm as you tackle the tasks of keeping a home running (such as gardening, cooking, cleaning, doing laundry, washing cars)?

Children need to make friends with work early in life and to understand that it is just as much a part of life as attachment, friends, and fun. Your job is to help structure, focus, and deepen their involvement in their work.

Work and Skill Are Part of Life (page 133)

Children tend to see work—the tasks of keeping a household running as well as the job that brings in the money—as something that takes you away from them, and that is a bad thing. So model interest in, involvement in, even frustration with your work both inside and outside the home. Let your children see that you love them, but you have a work life, too.

- **Values:** Your work is, at some level, tied into your values.

  — What kind of tasks within the home do you do, and why do you think they are important?

  — What kind of work outside the home, if any, do you do, and why do you think it is important?

— What might your young child understand about why you do what you do and why you think it's important?

- **Habits:** Model effective work ethics and habits.

    — What are you teaching-by-doing about being on time, finishing tasks, and following instructions?

— What household task do you (or could you) let your child do with minimum parental supervision? Picking up the play area, getting the cereal box off the shelf at the grocery store, and getting pajamas and perhaps even putting them on are a few possibilities. As your child gets older, what consequences might be appropriate for work not completed without supervision?

- **Attitudes:** Grumbling has been a part of work life ever since the Fall. So you can't ask children to whistle while they work, but you can require them to keep their protests respectful. Children also need to appreciate the value of what they're doing.

    — Consider the grumbling you do (if any). What attitude toward work are you modeling?

— What are you doing to show your children that you appreciate their beginning efforts to work around the house (picking up their toys, helping to set the table, sweeping the front walkway, and the like)?

- **Normalization:** Normalize work both inside and outside the home for your children. Let them know that you expect them to work most of their lives.

  — In which of your words and behaviors, if any, does your child see you living for weekends and vacation?

 — What work around the house can help your young child learn that work is a normal and ongoing aspect of life?

- **Delegation:** Children should be shouldering age-appropriate tasks.

 — What tasks are age-appropriate for your child?

  — What kind of enthusiastic commentary about those tasks will help your child realize that the family is a team and that the team works together?

- **Work and Money:** We don't believe in paying a child for chores. We suggest instead that, on a regular basis, you give your children some money not tied to chores. This can generally begin around kindergarten age when your child is learning about numbers and money issues.

— What are the benefits (long- and short-term) of this approach to work and money in your home?

— Although your child may be too young to be tithing, saving, and spending, take a few moments now to consider how and when you might want to implement such a program.

- **Skill:** In work, it's not enough to show up and participate. Results do matter. Help your child learn the importance of skill and achievement.

  — What problems can result from parents demanding too much? from parents being afraid to challenge their child? Which extreme (if either) did you grow up with, and what were the effects?

  — What can you do to be sure you're not asking either too little or too much of your child? What resources and reality checks can you consult?

- **Creativity and Problem Solving:** The heart of work is creating good things and solving problems. Getting children involved in tasks is inviting them to these fundamental aspects of work.

  — In what basic tasks like setting the table or putting away toys can you invite your young child to be creative?

— What can you do (or not do!) so that your child finds herself in the role of problem solver as she tackles an age-appropriate task? In what ways, for instance, can you empathize with the difficulty of the problem, but not rescue her and keep her from learning by doing the task at hand? What benefit comes to the child when you empathize rather than do the task for her?

- **Evaluation:** It helps kids to be graded on their performance. They need to experience both success and failure. Being graded helps them monitor their ways and make necessary corrections. It reinforces responsibility and punishes slothfulness.

    — Why isn't it helpful to eliminate failure from a child's experience?

— What does it mean to you to "fail well"—and what will you do to teach your child to fail well?

- **Competition:** Mastering tasks often involves some conflict with and comparison to other children. Help your child know how to compete well. However, competition should not be a big deal in the early years.

— What does "competing well" mean to you? As they grow older, what will you do to teach your children how to compete well and how to accept loss?

— What are you modeling about competition? about how to compete? and about how to accept loss? If he were older, in what scenes from your life would your child see you valuing relationship above competition?

- *Fears of Success and Failure:* Children will most likely struggle with fears of both doing well and failing in life. These two different struggles have much to do with their relationship with you as the parent.

    — As a child, did you fear success? Did you fear failure? If you answered yes to either question, how has that fear affected your life (and maybe still affects it)?

    — How can the unconditional love of their parents help keep these fears from taking root and later even incapacitating children?

Work and skill are part of life, and—especially since you're starting early— you can do much to help your child embrace work and succeed.

Developing Talents and Gifts (page 139)

Not only do you want to help your children learn how to integrate work into their lives, but you also want to help them with the specific interests, talents, gifts, and aptitudes God put into them in potential form. Parenting involves helping your children explore, discover, and develop those capacities that they will later enjoy and excel in.

- *Discovering Talents:* Within the souls of children are certain aptitudes waiting to emerge and bloom into talents and gifts. God has done his job, and your job is to invite your children to engage in various experiences so that you and they can figure out what they value, excel in, and love doing.

— Although you won't see these aptitudes emerge right away, you can think now about how you want to encourage them when they do become apparent. Remember John's dad's involved but hands-off way. What do you want to do and *not* do to help your children find out what they love and excel in?

— Keeping in mind that children work by playing, look around your home and wherever else your children spend a good amount of time. What interactive toys and art supplies encourage them to imagine and create? What might you do to make your children's environment stimulus-rich?

- **Development:** Invite your children to discover their interests. When they have latched onto some interest and have invested time and energy in it, challenge them to develop their talent.

— What lessons on encouraging your children to discover and pursue their interests does your own childhood experience offer? Jot down some ideas of things you want to do and maybe even don't want to do to help your children move from interest to competency.

— Preschoolers don't keep their (sometimes rather short-lived) interests a secret. What is yours interested in, or what has she been interested in? What kind of encouragement to pursue those interests did she receive or is she receiving?

- ***The Basics:*** All the while that you are guiding your children toward mastery in specialty areas, they should also be gaining competency in the universal areas of life that all adults need—areas such as academics, problem solving, social skills, language, hygiene and health, and home maintenance.

  — Why might it be easy for parents of a child gifted in some area to neglect these basic life skills? Why is that unwise and detrimental to the child?

  — Your preschooler has not yet entered the world of academics, but what are you doing (and could you be doing) to help him gain competence in the following areas? Be specific—it's not too early to start healthy life-long habits.

    Problem solving

    Social skills

    Language

    Hygiene and health

    Home maintenance

- **The Parent as Background:** Understand your parental role in helping children develop mastery. You are in the background, providing a structure for them to experience growth. Don't get caught feeling that your success is measured by your children's success.

  — Review the four words of caution listed on page 142 of the text. Which of the errors pointed out here have you seen or experienced? What resulted in the life of the child who suffered under these parental mistakes?

  — To which of these four dangers might you be most vulnerable as you parent your child? Think now about how to prevent that behavior.

It is a great calling to help your children discover their unique talents and grow competent in both those areas and life's tasks. Keep picturing them as future adults in whom you are investing time to help them prepare for entering the adult world.

Ages and Stages (page 142)

Kids are always working on something. They have God-given blueprints geared toward mastering life. Review the table on page 143 of the text, paying particular attention to the "Infancy," "Toddlerhood," and (if you have a five- or six-year-old) "Childhood" sections.

- What evidence do you see that your child is indeed working on these age-appropriate tasks?

- What items listed suggest that you can be helping your child master some of these basic tasks? What specific steps will you take?

As you watch your child tackle these age-appropriate tasks and encourage and assist along the way, again keep in mind that you are preparing her to enter the adult world as a competent and confident person.

Creating a Workaholic? (page 144)

Some parents fear that modeling, inviting, and challenging children to work will result in adults who are addicted to their job and have no other life. However, a healthily involved parent doesn't cause workaholism. If attachment, responsibility, and reality are all in their proper perspective in the child's character development, work capacities find their own place inside the child.

- Workaholics often find in their work respite from fears of closeness, an inability to make attachments, problems in setting limits with others, and anxieties about failure. How can healthily involved parenting help a child avoid these fears?

- Parents can't give what they don't have. How healthy is your approach to work? How balanced is your life? Does work help meet any unresolved needs or offer relief from the kinds of fears listed above? In essence, what are you modeling for your child?

Mastery of work is one of the most rewarding aspects of child rearing for the parent because it provides an opportunity to see measurable growth. But a working child isn't necessarily a moral child. In the next chapter, we will take a look at the important character task of conscience development.

Hands-on Exercise

If You Do One Thing Besides Pray . . .

Do you have a special way of telling each of your children that you will always love them no matter what they do? This week be intentional about letting each child know that powerful truth. Keep your words simple so that the message is clear. You might even come up with a between-you-and-her way of letting her know of your unconditional love. Could a quick wink when she catches your eye remind her? Be creative. As your child grows up, that gesture or phrase may become a real source of comfort for her.

Folded-Hands Exercise

"My help comes from the LORD . . ."

—PSALM 121:2

Almighty God, the truth that love and approval are different things is a powerful one, and it's one that your love helps me understand. You love me even when I sin, when I do and say things that you in your holiness don't approve of. I ask you to teach me to love my children with that kind of unconditional love. May I point them to your standards and mine for them, but may they always rest in our love for them.

I also ask you to give me wisdom and insight as my child's personality and interests, talents and skills emerge. Help me be a good steward of this precious treasure, teaching the basics of life at the same time I foster my child's unique abilities. Guide me as I guide my child toward mastery and competence. I pray in Jesus' name. Amen.

Making a Conscience
Morality

How is a child's conscience developed? Can it be injured? Can it be healed? Are there better ways to develop a conscience than others? What should you focus on as you think about moral development in your children? What morals are important? We will look at these issues in this chapter on conscience and morals.

What Is a Conscience? (page 146)

Defining conscience *is complicated for biblical theologians as well as psychologists. A child's moral awareness includes*

An understanding of right and wrong
The morals that will guide your child
An internal ability to weigh moral decisions
An ability to self-correct
A proper internal response to violating a standard
A desire to do right

• Where does the right or wrong in someone's conscience come from? What are you to feel when that standard is violated? Is the standard automatically right? Can you have a "wrong standard" in your conscience?

— Why are these questions important for parents to consider?

— If your child is past the infancy stage, what evidence of some of these items do you see in his behavior? Be specific and then, if you'd like, join the theologians and psychologists in considering the source of moral awareness and conscience. What ideas do you have?

If you send your child into adulthood with the above list, you will have done well. Let's look at how you can develop your child's moral awareness, what gets in the way, and what will help.

Three Big Things Worth Worrying About (page 147)

Parents worry. And the problem is not that parents worry; it's what parents worry about. Three things worth worrying about are that your children develop a conscience, the tone of the conscience, and the content and quality of the conscience.

- ***That They Develop a Conscience:*** "Moral development" refers to children developing both a moral awareness of right or wrong and the inclination to follow in the right direction and enforce internal consequences if they do wrong.

  — Your first task is to let your children know right from wrong. Setting limits for your children—identifying and defining things you allow and things you don't—can start sometime around the end of the child's first year. What limits have you set for your young child?

  — Explain in your own words why your no is a good thing.

— Are you at risk of setting too many rules? How can you consolidate or simplify the rules? Are you being too rigid to avoid being too lax? What might be a happy medium?

— A rule without enforcement teaches children that they are above the law and that morals are just suggestions. Are you consistent in your enforcement of the rules? What keeps you from being as consistent as you like? What help can you get if you would like to be more able to discipline and follow through on consequences?

- **The Tone of the Conscience:** The tone of your child's conscience will determine to some degree whether your child will follow it. Parents can build morals within their children, but if the tone of the child's conscience is angry, guilt-producing, and condemning, that conscience becomes the adversary.

  — The Bible teaches that we can live under the law (obey—or incur wrath, condemnation, and loss of love) or under grace (know love, forgiveness, and nurturing). What emotional tone are you offering your children when you discipline them? Review the descriptions of the tone of the law and the tone of grace (pages 149–50 in the text) before you answer this question.

  — "What was once outside becomes inside." What kind of parenting will provide a child with a conscience that is a friend? Apply your answer to a common situation in your home that requires you to discipline your child. What will you say, and how will you say it? What consequences will you enforce, and how will you do so?

- **The Content and Quality of the Conscience:** Now that you have decided to give your child a moral awareness and that it should be a gracious and loving enforcer, what are the laws of the land? On what are you going to focus? What kind of content is going to be written on the heart of your child? The content will change as the child grows up, but here are a few key principles for any age.

  — The Bible always teaches morality in the bigger context of hurting and rejecting God, hurting and splitting oneself, and hurting others. So *focus on the "whys" behind the rules; teach children that their behavior affects others*. In what ways can you apply this principle with your child? Be specific.

  — Morals are not killjoys. *Morals are to protect our lives and to ensure a good life*. They are the principles that undergird success in life, and reality teaches that truth. Reality consequences when they break a rule teach your children early that God's laws are there for a reason. *"If I do wrong, I suffer,"* the child learns. What reality consequences have you included (or could you include) in your plan for disciplining your child?

The content of the conscience will change as your child grows. But it should always be moving towards protecting relationships with God and others, as well as aligning oneself with the reality of God's created order. When you focus on relationship, reality issues, and reality consequences more than petty rules, you will have a child headed for a life of producing and protecting love as well as being able to function in reality.

The Process (page 154)

The moral functioning of a child is developmental, just like God's revelation to humankind: God gave the law to the children of Israel, and then in Jesus he fulfilled it with the principle of love and internal motivation. In the early stages, children understand the law.

- The sense of morality that children first have is based on their own pain and external consequences: "I feel bad, so I must have been bad." What, then, can uncomforted pain erroneously teach or at least reinforce in a very young child?

- Soon after infancy, a child's sense of morality changes to "I got spanked or scolded. Therefore I was bad." Morality is based on "what I get in trouble for." In light of this fact, why are consequences important in the shaping of a conscience?

As children mature and can understand higher forms of language, they begin to get their first view of real morality. They begin to understand right from wrong on a conceptual level. This perspective lasts through adolescence when they begin to understand it on a principle level.

Your Own Ten Commandments (page 155)

Children are building values and morality in the context of relationship. Your laws, as you teach them and as you live them, are being written on their hearts. These become part of their consciences through identification, imitation, modeling, and experience.

- **Identification** is the process by which children take in their parents at a very unconscious level.

— Are you seeing even your young child use some of the same expressions and gestures as you or your spouse? Give some examples.

— In the same way, children identify with their parents as moral agents. Children feel your attitudes toward things, and those attitudes will likely become part of them. What attitudes toward things do you want them to take in? What attitudes would you do well to change before your children begin to take them in and make them their own?

- *Imitation* is more active: children will imitate your behavior to learn how to behave.

— Give two or three examples of your child imitating how you speak, gesture, or deal with situations. At this young age, your child's imitation may, for instance, be shaving like Daddy or wearing Mommy's high heels.

— What forms of speech, gestures, or behaviors might you want to change in light of the little sponge now living in your home?

- *Modeling* is the taking on of roles and abilities, such as the role of being male or female and the ability to treat people nicely or poorly.

— Children model your compassion, forgiveness, and sacrifice, and they also model your harshness, anger, and self-centeredness. What you show your children is what they become. What kind of warning, if any, do you find in these statements?

— In what ways are you showing your child how to be a moral person? Be specific.

— Where, if at all, are you saying one thing but modeling another?

• Children will not only imitate you, but also ***experience*** you directly. Just as God gave his family (the children of Israel) a set of commandments to follow, parents give their family their own set. It is given not in stone, but with experience.

— Remember the examples of relational theology some people learned growing up? (See page 157 of the text.) What would you add to the list? Which items, if any, are lessons you learned?

— Now consider yourself as parent. What relational theology are you beginning to teach your child?

— Two parents form a conscience. If both parents are not on the same page, a child gets a "split conscience." How much in sync are you and your spouse as you serve as the external conscience for your children? Where do you need to be more in line with each other—in tone? in content? in quality? What will you do to improve your alignment? Be specific.

Remember, no matter what you believe, how you relate to your children is forming their own conscience. Their brains are recording as rules your responses to them.

Some Good Values (page 159)

Review the list of good values to instill in your children (page 159 in the text). The Bible teaches that these are the basic values that life in God is built upon. Take time—now and regularly as your child grows up—to consider each value listed.

- What are you teaching your children about each value through your words—and what do you want to be teaching them? What will you do to teach those lessons?

- What are you teaching your children about each of these values by your actions—and what do you want to be teaching them? What will you do to teach those lessons?

In the final analysis, conscience is an important aspect of parenting. But to just give a child rules falls short of a biblical view of conscience. Make sure that rules are focused on love, corrected by love, and built in the context of love. If they are, your child will one day thank you for all the discipline along the way.

In the next chapter we will look at the deepest morality: a child's connection to God.

Hands-on Exercise

If You Do One Thing Besides Pray . . .

Make an appointment or grab a cup of coffee with a dad or mom farther down the parenting road whose children are leading godly, moral lives. Get some tips from them. Learn from their mistakes. And ask any questions you may have.

Folded-Hands Exercise

"My help comes from the LORD . . ."

—PSALM 121:2

Almighty God, you are clear in your Word that there are two ways of living—under the law or under grace. I ask you to help the tone in our home to be one of grace, and I acknowledge that I can't do that without your Spirit working in me. Be at work, I pray, transforming the angry, harsh, condemning, guilt-producing, and alienating words and ways I have and the danger of withholding love from my children based on their performance. And, Father, replace those with manifestations of your grace—with an ability to be loving, nurturing, and forgiving, to offer an unconditional love that builds relationship and empowers my children. I need you and the wisdom you can provide me as I face the challenge of making a healthy and godly conscience in my children. I pray in Jesus' name. Amen.

Nine

Connecting to God
Worship and Spiritual Life

Parenting Principles

- A child's spiritual life needs to be centered around connecting to God as the Author of reality.
- Parents need to present to their children spiritual life integrated with everyday life.
- Parents need to teach kids the spiritual disciplines and give them experiences to internalize them.

Concerned not only about the cultural and political shifts of the late sixties but the spiritual problems as well, John's dad volunteered to teach Sunday school to the teens in our church. Like him, you may have a deep desire to foster your child's spiritual life, but you wonder where to begin. This chapter resolves this tension by dealing with two aspects—being involved and having a structure in which to operate.

Character and Spirituality (page 162)

Your child's spiritual life is a fundamental part of total character development. Remember that growing character helps your child function as an adult in the world.

- Children demand that life adapt to them, while mature adults adapt themselves to the realities of life. So, to grow up, your children need to order their lives around the Author of reality. God has designed your children—and reality—to operate in certain ways within certain parameters. Finding and responding to God's statutes and ways becomes the key to growing up.

— As your children grow up, what will they see in you as to what ordering one's life around the Author of reality looks like? Will they see God as the center of your life? Will they see you in relationship with him?

— As you were growing up, how did you learn God's statutes and ways— and how have you responded to them through the years?

• You may know loving, hardworking, and reality-based people who have no spiritual life or interests, who don't experience God as the source of life. You may also know highly religious folks who know the Bible well and use God talk, but their everyday lives don't reflect what they know. For them, the center of what makes them tick is not connected to the rest of "real" life.

— What might a parent be doing that contributes to each of these two possibilities?

— What might a parent do to prevent these two possibilities and raise a child who experiences God as the source of life, whose everyday life reflects a personal knowledge of Jesus?

Parents cannot separate their children's spiritual life from the rest of life. Our spiritual life is meant to be integrated into all the aspects of our relationships and tasks. Spiritual character growth therefore involves much more than religious training; it involves helping the child experience that the essence of existence is spiritual.

Creating a Place for Relationship to Grow (page 163)

Life begins with a relationship, and spiritual life is no exception. It begins with a relationship between your child and God. The development of a spiritual relationship is extremely important during the first few years of life. Children who learn early who God is and how he wants to be with them are more able to integrate his reality into the rest of their years.

- A relationship requires two willing parties. You can't force your child to develop a relationship with God. God invites, but does not force himself on you or your child (Revelation 3:20).

  — God has arranged things so that children have a voice as to when they are ready to address him. Why is this both sobering and freeing?

  — Your task is to do background work for your child's encounter with God, to create a context that fosters connectedness to God. Before looking closely at some ways to do so, consider what you are doing even now to create optimal conditions for your child to meet and love God (Hebrews 11:6). Are you, for instance, praying aloud with your infant? Are you softly singing some of the great hymns as lullabies? Give a few examples from your everyday life as a parent.

- ***Seeing the Eternal in the Everyday:*** Your child needs to approach life as if it were eternal; this is fundamental in the quest for God. One of the advantages you have in developing your child's spiritual life is that children are open to the transcendent. The very dependency of children lends itself to their accepting a world beyond their understanding, with rules they can't comprehend.

— Prepare now to help your children see the eternal in the everyday parts of life. What about your day can you point out to your child as evidence that God exists and cares? Where do you see the eternal in the everyday? Help your child see, for instance, how God brings friends around us, keeps us safe in the car, provides good weather for fun outings, or answers the prayer you prayed with your child. Ask the Lord to give you eyes to see his active presence and involvement in your life.

— Also prepare now to help your child experience that the rules in both the seen and the unseen worlds are similar, that principles such as love, faithfulness, honesty, and ownership work in both worlds. What current situation in your life gives you the opportunity to make this point? Also, spend some time asking the Lord to show you where you are not living in this world according to the rules of the unseen world, the rules and principles he established for both.

- **Seeing God as the Source of All Good Things:** Children need to understand that, while God wants them to follow his ways, he first wants to give them the good things they need.

  — What would you like to do and say to help your child learn "that God is a better parent . . . than [you] are"?

— Your child needs to see that you are a better parent by virtue of being connected to God. When has being in prayer, worship, or Bible study clearly given what you need to better love your child? Be specific about the time and, in order to experience it regularly, note what helped make it especially significant for you and the Lord.

— What, if anything, has your child seen in you about how God gives good things (such as peace, hope, and strength) in the midst of hard times?

 — In the last few weeks, when could your child have seen in your life that good things happen when people spend time with God, even though suffering happens, too?

- **Life Works Better Living It God's Way:** God provides your children with all the good things they need to live, but in doing so, he also requires them to order their lives around his ways. The Bible contains those ways: truth exists in God's commands, laws, and principles for conducting our lives. Your children need to understand and experience these truths (Psalm 1:2).

  — When have you experienced for yourself the truth that obedience to God's ways helps us, that spiritual growth and development both prosper and preserve life (Deuteronomy 6:24)? Be specific.

 — In what common situation in a preschooler's life can you begin to teach your child that God's ways help us? What will you do and say, for instance, the next time your toddler doesn't want to share?

— What are you doing regularly to get to know God's Word, Christian theology, and biblical principles? What are you doing (or could you be doing) to introduce your preschooler to the Bible and God's ways as well as to the importance of knowing his Word and his truth? Having fun with Bible stories (using hand motions for the thunder and lightning of Jonah's storm; changing your voice to be young David and huge Goliath) can help your child look forward to reading the Scriptures with you.

- ***The Spiritual Disciplines and Their Purpose:*** Learning the truths and principles is not enough for your children's spiritual development. Parenting also involves helping children internalize the disciplines of spiritual life. Spiritual disciplines—like prayer, fellowship, and the study of, the memorization of, and meditation on God's Word—are the traditional activities people of faith have entered into for many years as a way to connect with God.

    — What spiritual disciplines are a nurturing habit for you? Which ones do you need to better integrate in your life, especially now that you have a little one watching you?

    — What are you doing (and what else can you do) to practice the various spiritual disciplines with your children? What Bible storybooks, for instance, do you have around? What Sunday school program does your child attend? What family mealtime rituals can you start? What special weekly time for family worship or devotionals can you set into place?

Your Faith Matters to Your Child's Faith (page 169)

More than any other character capacity, spiritual development is "caught" more than taught. Children will internalize more of what their parents are with God and with them than what their parents teach.

- What fellow believer can help you to see what kind of faith you model to people around you? Talk to that person about your strengths as well as your weaknesses and ask for prayer as you seek to lead a life of faith that you want your children to "catch" and follow.

- What stories of your own doubts, struggles with God, failings to be the person he wants you to be will you regularly share with your children as they grow up? How will you let them see that a relationship with God, like a relationship with anyone, takes time, has conflict, and requires work?

The Image of God Issue (page 170)

Children internalize experiences of their parents to form an image of God; however, other important factors (interpretation of life events, other realities, the ability to distinguish between human and divine, and change and growth) play a part in the development of a child's image of God.

- How did your impression of your parents form or impact your image of God for good or bad? What contributed to your growing beyond that image to a more mature and biblical understanding of God?

- Your children were created to seek and find God. What opportunities to draw close to God are you giving your child? What experiences (for example, being around good people who love our good God) do you want to be sure to provide your children as they grow up?

From Immature to Mature Dependency (page 171)

Your role of parent is temporary; God's is not. Your child was designed to be God's kid forever (John 14:23). So you need to order your children's earthly child-parent relationship differently from their heavenly one. While you are helping them to need you less, you are helping them need God more.

- What were some key events in your life that helped you transition from dependence on parents to dependence on the Lord? What lessons for parenting does your own experience provide you?

- Review the chart of age-appropriate capacities and spiritual needs (pages 172–74 in the text) to see what tasks are yours as you help your child make a shift from immature to mature dependency on God the Father. In what ways, for instance, does your infant experience safety and love from you? What kind of family worship is your toddler involved in? What simple Bible stories and songs are in your child's repertoire? In what teaching times, worship and prayer experiences, and family ministry activities are you involving your preschooler?

The Age of Faith? (page 174)

Parents struggle with the age-old question of when and how to help their child make a decision of faith. Only God knows the child's heart and readiness. As well, only he knows the hour and day that our lives will be required of us (Luke 12:20). And so parents need to rest in the reality of God's love, his deep and abiding love for their child (2 Peter 3:9).

- What can you do to help your children begin to understand these basic gospel truths so that they can make an authentic decision for Christ?

     The existence and love of God (as we've said, point out his involvement in your everyday life)

The reality of our sinful state (preschoolers can understand the struggle of wanting to do the right thing but being unable to do so)

The penalty of sin and God's provision through the death of Christ (Easter is a great opportunity for this)

The requirement of accepting Christ personally (talk about the difference between knowing *about* God and knowing God)

As you answer this question, keep in mind the age-appropriate capacities and spiritual needs of your child (see again pages 172–74 in the text).

- A home where life in Christ is integrated with going to work, making dinner, taking out the trash, and interacting with family members is a good context for encouraging your children to commit themselves to Christ as their Savior and Lord. While your child is still young, determine where you can better integrate your faith with your day-to-day life.

- Starting now, be a student of your children. Get to know each one's character (is he private or outgoing? does she want to figure things out for herself or is she always teachable?) so that you will have a better idea of your role in inviting them to name Jesus as their Savior and Lord.

Your Father in heaven wants a relationship with your child. Ask him daily how you can help and when you need to get out of the way for this process to occur in his time.

Having considered the six character traits every child needs, we will now look at how parents are involved differently in different periods of their children's lives. Part 3 focuses on older children, but you will benefit from reading that section now. After all, you are laying the foundation for the parenting you will need to do in the future.

Hands-on Exercise

If You Do One Thing Besides Pray . . .

As we have stated, your faith matters to your child's faith. So, while your child is young, work on strengthening your faith in the Lord so that you are walking your talk and modeling a vibrant faith in God that can be caught even as it is taught.

Where do you need to better walk your talk?

What regular Bible study or prayer group offers you support, accountability, and growth opportunities?

In what ways and at what times is worship a regular part of your life?

What regular prayer appointments with God do you keep?

In what ways are you serving the Lord and his people?

How are you giving of your treasures, talents, and time for his kingdom?

Who might serve as a spiritual mentor for you? Ideally that person would be someone whose older children have chosen for themselves to walk with the Lord.

Ask the Lord to help you see the eternal in the everyday, to see him as the Source of all good things, and to live life his way.

Folded-Hands Exercise

"My help comes from the LORD . . ."

—PSALM 121:2

Almighty God, it is very sobering to realize that one's faith in you is more caught than taught. What will my young child see in me and in my walk with you? Teach me, I pray, to turn to you and depend on you in all areas of my life. Use the time I spend with you to make me a better parent. And help my relationship with you stay fresh, not become formal and stiff . . . my prayers real, not rote . . . and my Bible study a life-source, not a mere duty. Finally, Lord, I ask you to help my children come to the point of owning their own faith—of coming to know you and love you and serve you—not merely piggybacking on my faith but coming to faith in Jesus because they have personally encountered you, wrestled with you, acknowledged their sin, and accepted your love. I pray in the name of Jesus, your ultimate gift of love to me and my child. Amen.

Part Three

Working Yourself Out of a Job

Ten

Preparing Them for Life on Their Own

Even if parenting an adolescent seems a long way off, take time to read through the two chapters in this section because what you are doing now is laying the foundation for then! The questions with the hand icon apply to your life today. Intentional parenting now can help life be easier for you and your child during the teenage years.

— Parenting Principles —

- Adolescence is a reworking of past developmental issues in a new context.
- Parents need to set limits on how far a child can go in working out these issues.
- The goal of adolescence is responsible independence, but parents need to be guiding the process.

Henry's parents saw adolescence as a time-limited opportunity to prepare me to be on my own, and I'm grateful for what they did. Other parents, by their actions, say, "You are not on your own, so this is what you will do." And still others never offer any kind of parental limit. As you will see in this sneak preview of what's ahead in your parenting, adolescence is a season of paradoxes for child as well as Mom and Dad.

The Big Picture (page 180)

To really understand adolescence, you need to stand back and understand first the big picture of how a child develops into an adult. Then you will understand adolescence as something both essential and important.

- Review "The Big Picture" overview of child development (pages 180–83).

— In a sense, how is parenting a two-year-old like parenting an adolescent?

— What parallel issues do kids encounter in the early-elementary years and their adolescence?

Adolescence is a time when all of the past developmental issues (listed on page 182 of the text) are reworked in a different context. Your child will work out those issues more independently in preparation for adulthood. Let's consider each item on the list.

Trust and Dependency (page 183)

In teenagers, learning trust and dependency is more complicated than it is for an infant. But what parents of young children do is lay a foundation for them to learn trust and dependency all over again in some different ways when they are adolescents.

• What have you done and are you doing to help your child trust you and your spouse? In what ways do you connect with your child? In what ways do you soothe him?

• Adolescents put more trust into others than their parents as one way of establishing independence. In what ways do you see your young child making an effort to establish some independence?

Independence and Autonomy (page 187)

One parent described adolescence as the terrible twos all over again, but this time in a bigger body. We personally don't see either time period as "terrible," but each one can be full of difficulty if you don't recognize the important stage of independence, separateness, and autonomy that a child is going through.

- Parents of preschoolers as well as parents of adolescents can participate in their child's emerging autonomy by being proactive. What, for instance, can you do to give your two- or three-year-old some responsibility at home? your four-, five-, or six-year-old?

- In what areas is your child wanting independence (choice of clothes he wears, "menu planning," arranging his room the way he wants it—untidy though it be)? What will you do to encourage and enable this growing independence?

- *Partnering in independence and autonomy means to think always about your children guarding and managing themselves at the appropriate level. Give them enough space to fail and then manage the failure with nurture, empowerment, support, discipline, and correction.*

  —In what ways can you apply this advice to parents of teens to your own situation as a parent of a preschooler? Be specific about one or two instances when you will give them space to fail and how you will manage that failure.

Limits and Authority (page 192)

It is important to let children gradually become independent and more autonomous, but you need to protect them and manage them in the process.

- When have you seen your preschooler act as if she knows everything or insist that "I'm a big girl! I do it myself!"? How did you respond?

- Why is "freedom within limits" a good rule of thumb for you, whatever your child's age?

- Review the discussion of reality limits, "past-their-ability" limits, and moral/spiritual/interpersonal limits (pages 193–94 in the text). Give two or three examples in each category of how these categories are relevant and helpful as you parent your preschooler.

Again, adolescence is a time when all of the past developmental issues are reworked in a different context. Preschoolers are working these issues out for the first time. They need their parents to stay close now just as they will need you to in ten years or so—only they won't necessarily be able to express that need very clearly either time!

In the next chapter, we will discuss specific things that many parents of teenagers ask about.

Hands-on Exercise

If You Do One Thing Besides Pray . . .

Maybe it's time to talk to a parent of a teenager who seems to be on the right track. Let the focus of your conversation be "What, if anything, can I be doing now to smooth the road of adolescence for my child . . . for myself . . . for our relationship as parent-child?" Perhaps someone else's Monday-morning-quarterbacking will give you some insight and tips.

Folded-Hands Exercise

"My help comes from the LORD . . ."

—PSALM 121:2

Lord, I find real comfort in reminding myself that, just as you are with me now, you will be with me as I parent an adolescent—and every step in between! This discussion has also reminded me that the challenges of each day are challenge enough. Teach me even now to look to you for all I need—wisdom, patience, self-control, love—a day at a time as I raise the child you have entrusted to me. It is an overwhelming responsibility, but you don't leave me alone in it—and you never will. Keep me mindful of the resources your Holy Spirit and your written Word are for me, so that I will never be trying to do this crucial job in my own power or might. I pray in Jesus' name. Amen.

——— Eleven ———

A Look into the Future

Even if parenting an adolescent seems a long way off, take time to read through this chapter because what you are doing now is laying the foundation for then! The questions with the hand icon apply to your life today. Intentional parenting now can help life be easier for you and your child during the teenage years.

Parenting Principles

- Parents need to provide principles to help kids make good decisions in areas such as music, clothing, sex, and substances.
- During these years, parents need to remember to use grace, truth, and time and to be flexible.
- Parents need to have their own limits and the proper stance toward pleasure to develop delay of gratification in their teens.

We are strong believers in principles, because principles tell you how to handle almost any situation. So, we usually do not talk about "how to handle" specifics. But some specific situations are very common in dealing with teens.

Music (page 195)

- What value is there in letting your children have their own musical choices in terms of style, beat, kind, and decibel level?

- What kinds of limits are essential? What limits does the Golden Rule suggest?

- What kind of homework does a parent have to do before limiting a teen's music?

- What can you do now to start laying the groundwork for these limits?

Hair, Clothes, Earrings, Appearance (page 195)

- What are some appropriate limits in this category—and why are they appropriate?

- Again, what kind of homework does a parent have to do before limiting a young person's dress?

- What can you do now to start laying the groundwork for these limits?

Curfew (page 196)

- Describe how freedom within limits can work when it comes to setting a curfew.

• What does it mean that "the limit was made for your child, not your child for the limit"? Explain, using a hypothetical or real-life situation.

Spirituality (page 196)

• Comment on the value of setting this limit for a young adult: "Our family reserves this time for God. You don't have to go to church if you don't want to, but you can't do anything else either."

 • What are you doing now to expose your young child to God and to your faith and beliefs?

 • What are you doing now to live out your spiritual values of love, faithfulness, honesty, compassion, forgiveness, stewardship of talents and life, and hope?

Sex and Substances (page 197)

 • What is your plan for educating your child about sex and substances?

• In talking about sexuality, what approach will you take to avoid sending messages about guilt and shame?

- When addressing substances (tobacco, alcohol, marijuana, and harder stuff), what kind of good teaching do you want to provide? What kind of modeling are you doing at home even now?

Studies (page 199)

- What do you plan to expect from your children in the way of academics, grades, and school involvement when they are in junior high school and high school?

- What kinds of consequences may you need to use to enforce your standards?

In all of these areas—music, appearance, curfew, spirituality, sex and substances, and studies—the message is simple and the ingredients are clear. And the message and ingredients are relevant even now when your child is young.

The message is that "some things are dangerous, so stay away from them; some things are not wise, so do not do them; some things are not moral, so avoid them; and you are in charge until you prove you cannot be."

The ingredients of parenting at this stage are grace (show your children that you are for them); truth (show them what is right and enforce it with correction, limits, and reality consequences); time (parenting is a process); and flexibility (in this dance, you and your child are both changing your roles).

Living with and Accepting Imperfection in Themselves and Others (page 200)

Teens have totally unrealistic standards for themselves and sometimes for others. They go up and down with their own failures and successes. Help them to accept themselves as they are with a goal of always getting better.

- What do you remember of this roller-coaster ride? You might want to write down some thoughts now. They may help you empathize with your child ten years from now (if not before!).

- The best defense against imperfection is love. To the degree that your children feel loved, they will be able to accept their imperfections. Do not devalue their feelings, but empathize and accept them. Give them lots of positive feedback on their strengths and talents.

— What helps you accept your imperfections? What are you teaching your children about accepting one's own imperfections by your example?

— In what ways are you already showing your child that you love her, imperfections included?

— "You don't have to become a teenager to deal with one!" In what ways, if any, is this advice (with the change of the word *teenager* to *preschooler*) applicable to the parent of an easily frustrated two-year-old, an "I-want-to-do-it-myself" three-year-old, a confident preschooler, and an energetic kindergartner?

Frustration, Tolerance, and Delay of Gratification (page 201)

- Delay of gratification comes from a parent having limits and the proper stance toward pleasure. Teach your children that pleasure is good, but for pleasure that lasts, we have to work first.

- How did you learn delay of gratification as you were growing up? What lesson(s), if any, do you clearly remember?

- What steps toward learning frustration, tolerance, and delay of gratification can you offer your preschooler? What coaching can you offer when her young friend is taking a long turn with the prized toy? When can you help your child practice waiting for that ice cream cone or the anticipated trip to the toy store?

Children need to learn to delay gratification until they do their part. Encourage and help them along the way, without enabling them by bailing them out and making life seem easier than it really is. Help them learn to work first and play later. The principle will serve them for a lifetime.

Social Group Demands and Interpersonal Skills (page 202)

Teens should be involved in large group activities as well as dating and opposite-sex relationships. Healthy teens also have a clan that they run around with.

- Start now getting your children used to playing at home with their friends. What are you doing to make your home a friendly place? What friends or play group do you regularly have over?

- What lessons in interpersonal skills (such as sharing, taking turns, not being bossy) do these play times give you the opportunity to teach and reinforce?

From the start, help your children avoid patterns that may someday cost them friendships.

Talents, Abilities, and Interests (page 203)

Consider the following points about talents, abilities, and interests that parents can focus on to help their teen develop.

- Which of these guidelines did your parents follow when you were growing up? How did you benefit? Be specific.

    1. Make sure your children's interests are theirs, not yours.

    2. Support them in what they do choose.

    3. Require them to stick it out, especially if you're paying for it.

    4. Expose them to a lot of choices and, to an extent, help in creating opportunities.

    5. Share activities and skills with your children.

- Which of these bits of parental advice can you begin acting on to some degree even now?

The Result (page 204)

If parents of a teen do all that these two chapters outline, then they will have a new person at the end of the process. They will have a friend for life—one of whom they can be proud and whom they can watch unfold as God directs her steps into the future.

- If you and your parents are friends, to what do you attribute that wonderful outcome? Learn from your own experience.

- If you and your parents aren't friends, what interfered along the way? Again, learn from your own experience.

If parents give their teens the process of freedom, discipline, love, support, and forgiveness to help them become their own people, that is something to be proud of as they let go and retire from their job as parent.

Hands-on Exercise

If You Do One Thing Besides Pray . . .

At this point of your parenting journey, as you consider the teen issues mentioned in this chapter—music; hair, clothes, appearance; spirituality; sex and substances; accepting imperfection in oneself; frustration tolerance and delay of gratification; social group; and talents, abilities, and interests—you may feel overwhelmed by the "What are you doing now?" questions. Choose one area to focus on this week and do something with your preschooler to help her grow in that area. Here are some ideas:

- Read together Robert Kraus's *Leo the Late Bloomer* (HarperCollins) to encourage your preschooler to accept imperfection in herself—and then share a story about yourself so that you can model thatimportant ability.
- Sow seeds of pride in appearance by emphasizing how important it is to dress up for church on Sunday.
- If you're potty training,remind her that private parts aren't for just anybody to touch.
- If your older preschooler is asking questions, share appropriate parts of Peter Mayle's *Where Did I Come From?* (Carol Publishing Group).
- Turn a question("What is that person drinking?" or "What is that a picture of?") into a teachable moment by explaining a little about the dangers of alcohol or cigarettes.
- Take her to the ballet, a concert, or the high-school soccer game, an activity that reflects an area where you've noticed a talent beginning to emerge or in which she's expressed an interest.
- Or, in a light-hearted, playful voice, give your preschooler the opportunity to ask you about anything in the whole wide world—and let this question become a regular part of your conversations, part of a pattern of open communication that you would like to have last her whole life long.

Folded-Hands Exercise

"My help comes from the LORD . . ."

—PSALM 121:2

"You don't have to become a teenager to deal with one!" That bit of wisdom works just as well for me—"I don't have to become a preschooler to deal with one!" But I know my limitations. So, Holy Spirit, I pray that you will grant me the grace and wisdom, the patience and love I need to effectively parent my easily frustrated two-year-old, my "I want to do it myself" three-year-old, my confident preschooler, or my energetic kindergartner. And bless my efforts, Lord, so that my child will become—by your grace—a teenager who knows you and relies on you in the face of the challenges he will face. I pray in Jesus' name. Amen.

Part Four

Dealing with Special Circumstances

—— Twelve ——

Understanding Temperaments

Parenting Principles

- Temperament is an inborn style of relating to the world, and that style is different in different children.
- Character is the ability to function in life. It is more important than temperament.
- Temperament should not excuse improper behavior; it can be modified with experience.

Temperament has to do with certain categories of inborn traits that cause people to respond differently to life. This may include tendencies toward introversion or extroversion and activity or passivity, for example. Many parents wonder about how to deal with temperaments.

Temperament Is Not Character (page 207)

Temperament is a style of relating to the world: individual differences, from energy level to academic interests, make up your child's unique soul. Character, however, is not a style: character is a set of abilities necessary to function in the world. Character is neither an option nor an alternative. It is a requirement for survival. Character comes first and style second.

- If you have brothers and sisters, what different temperaments are represented among you? Is one outgoing and one more reserved? Is one more active and another more passive? How, if at all, did your parents compensate for that—or how could they have done so?

- You need to help your children mature in all of the character traits we have written about in this book. But take their individuality into consideration as you do.

  — Make this statement more personal. What, for instance, does your sensitive child need in the way of correction? your turbo-charged child?

  — Describe your child's temperament. What have you noticed so far? How will you adjust your parenting to your child's temperament while teaching the essentials of character? Share some initial ideas.

Whatever your child's temperament, the task of learning responsibility is the same. All kids, whatever their style, need to take ownership of their lives.

- One of the difficulties of parenting is that your child needs your help in all areas of character, but you most likely won't excel in all. Your ability in each area is not the same.

  — In which of the following areas do you feel strong and able to parent? Jot down an idea or two for starting to build that aspect of character into your preschooler.

  Attachment

  Responsibility

  Reality

  Competence

  Morality

  Worship and Spiritual Life

— Which of these six aspects of character are areas that you need to or would like to strengthen? What will you do toward that end?

We can't overemphasize the importance of finding help from others for your weak areas. Your parenting experiences will expose these weaknesses. When that happens, turn to God, his resources, and his people for relationship, healing, and growth.

How to Tell the Difference (page 209)

It is sometimes difficult to tell if a problem is temperament-influenced or character-based because the outworking of each is similar. You may notice, for example, that your four-year-old boy is more energetic and assertive than his playmates. He may have a hard time sitting still, paying attention to instructions, and keeping his hands to himself. Some of this behavior may be due to his more active temperament; he is just wired to be more active, rather than calm and docile. But some of this behavior may also be due to a lack of structure and consequences that can help him settle down. No one knows what percentage is one or the other.

The important thing is to provide enough boundaries in your child's experience for him to be able to be the active or calm child God intended, not someone who learns to excuse his inappropriate behavior by saying, "That's just the way I am."

Again, it is sometimes difficult to tell whether a problem is temperament- or character-based. An expert (such as a teacher or psychologist) can be helpful, but we want to point out a basic difference in temperament-influenced behavior and character-based issues: When character issues are resolved, the remaining temperament issues don't tend to be a major problem.

- Read that statement again: When character issues are resolved, the remaining temperament issues don't tend to be a major problem. When, if ever, have you seen the truth of this statement in real life? (Consider the example given above.) More specifically, when have you seen the resolution of a character issue bring a temperament more into the range of "normal" or acceptable?

- If you see in your child a tendency that concerns you, a good rule of thumb is to investigate it first as a character issue.

  — Review the six questions listed on pages 209–10 in the text and those listed below.
  Is your child's behavior a way to seek attachment and relationship?
  Does it show a lack of personal boundaries and responsibility?
  Is your child trying to cover up weakness and vulnerability by being aggressive?
  Could your child's behavior be a response to her inner perfectionism?

    Why does a *yes* answer to any of these questions suggest a character issue—a matter of attachment, responsibility, reality, competence, morality, or worship and spiritual life—rather than a temperament issue?

  — If you can answer *yes* to any of the questions, what could you as a parent do to address the character problem you have just identified in your child? Think about what you've been learning in the text and this workbook.

Most of the time a child's behavioral problem is a matter of character, especially with regard to disruptive problems. Differences in temperaments don't tend to be as extreme.

So What? (page 210)

Now let's imagine some children who are struggling with an issue that is 0 percent character and 100 percent temperament. If that is the case, even though their temperament is not their fault, they are increasingly responsible for dealing with it as they grow up.

- What aspects of your temperament have you struggled to become responsible for rather than simply falling back on "I can't help it. That's just how I am"? What has helped you be victorious in that struggle that might help your child do the same?

- When do parents deal with temperament as a problem, not a "way of being"? Here is the rule: Deal with temperament when it inhibits growth in attachment, responsibility or ownership, reality, competence, morality, or worship and spiritual life—the six aspects of character growth.

— Where, if at all, is your child's temperament inhibiting development in one of the six areas of character growth we have been considering? Your toddler, for example, may by nature be more energetic than other children, so he may need you to help him learn self-control by giving him a strong but loving set of boundaries and consequences.

— Review the chapter in the text that addresses that particular aspect of character growth. What can you do to help your child? What *will* you do to help your child?

— How will relationship with you help your child deal with this aspect of character growth? Remember that relationship is key!

Styles and temperaments can be modified with experience. Research has shown that environment has a powerful effect even on inborn traits. This is a testimony to the redemptive work of God: our traits don't determine our lives.

The Strong-willed Child (page 211)

Some parents avoid confronting the determination of strong-willed children to have life their own way. They don't want to squelch these children's will or discourage them from being decisive. At the same time, they are concerned about helping the children mind them and learn obedience.

- Is yours a strong-willed child? Give some specific evidence supporting why you answered the question the way you did.

- In what ways can the following parental tools help soften that strong will? Be specific.

Love

Empathy

Correction

Experience

Consequences

We have seen many examples where people have been able to make significant changes in their kids' lives using these principles.

The strong-willed child's power should end where the family's peace of mind begins.

Hands-on Exercise

If You Do One Thing Besides Pray . . .

Spend some time working specifically on a weak area in your own character so that you can be more effective in helping your child develop in that aspect. Develop a plan of action and then do it.

Folded-Hands Exercise

"My help comes from the LORD . . ."

—PSALM 121:2

Almighty God, you knit together my child. You know my child well. You created that unique soul, temperament, personality . . . and you gave me the privilege of being a parent to that child. Lord, sometimes as a parent I'm at a loss about whether I'm dealing with a character problem or a temperament problem. Thank you that you give wisdom when we ask—I'm asking! Thank you that you bless us with creativity when we need to solve problems—I'm in need! And thank you that you are strong when I am weak—and I'm weak in certain aspects of character, but I still need my kids to learn those.

Please, Lord, as I walk this parenting road, may I know your presence with me in a very tangible, real way so that I may have insight into my kids (is the situation a matter of temperament or character?) and wisdom about how to resolve that issue and raise them to please and honor you. Thank you that you redeem my mistakes and my child's weaknesses in temperament and character flaws. I pray in Jesus' name. Amen.

—— Thirteen ——

Parenting on Your Own

Even if you're married, be sure to work through the "When to Get Help" section that begins on page 216. It's important for all parents to know when they are dealing with a parenting problem that is beyond their resources.

Parenting Principles

- Single parenting has its own set of challenges as the parent makes sure that the child is getting the resources that two parents would normally provide.
- Parents (single or otherwise) need to first evaluate the severity of their children's problems and then decide how to approach those problems.
- God is especially accessible to assist the child of the single parent (Psalm 68:5).

The other material in this workbook certainly applies to you, but we wanted to include a special section that speaks to the particular challenges you face as a single parent. Parenting on your own is very difficult and brings its own set of problems. If this is your situation, our hearts go out to you as you deal with both personal and parenting losses. Know, however, that God understands your struggle and that he is close to the brokenhearted (Psalm 34:18).

The Conditions (page 213)

To help you parent your children, we are going to look at some of the main conditions a two-parent household has the advantage of being able to deal with. Then, with each condition, we will provide suggestions on how you as a single parent can help your child in these areas.

• **Children ideally need two parents to meet their varied needs.**

— What do you see as your strengths and your weaknesses? Be sure to specifically address the six aspects of character we have been considering.

— What healthy relationships are you (or could you become) involved in? Among these people, whom can you ask to help you in the areas where you are weak?

 • **Children are demanding.**

— What time away from your child do you have available to you?

— What co-op baby-sitting with other parents can you become involved in?

— What friends or family members can assist you so that you come back to your child refreshed and looking forward to connecting with him?

• **Parenting is basically relationship.**

 — What models of healthy relationship do you or could you make available to your child?

— What are you doing to keep at bay the enemies of isolation and self-sufficiency?

— What regular times do you set aside to invest in relationship for yourself?

- **Two parents help the child enter the world of other people.**

   — Late in the second year of a child's life, Father plays a more central role than before and helps the child move out of his honeymoon with Mom. Are you and your child still honeymooning? Are you finding yourself feeling protective of your child (a very natural maternal feeling) and having a hard time letting your child invest in other people? Why do you need to let go and free your child to learn to invest in and trust other people?

   — Especially in your child's younger years, single moms need to find stable, healthy men whom they aren't dating to help the child enter the world of other people. Who in your life falls into that category—or where might you get to know such a person?

- **Two parents help the child move out of self-centeredness.**

   — Whom do your children see you loving besides them? Why is this important for your children?

— What adults besides you does your child eat, play, work, and relax with? If that's not a regular part of your routine, what specific step will you take toward that goal this week? Put differently, whom will you invite over this weekend to share a picnic or play in the park?

• ***Parents also provide a check and balance on each other.***

— All of us parents have our blind spots. Whom do you let close enough to see your blind spots and help you work on your parenting faults?

— What good support groups for single parents are available to you? Look into MOPS (Mothers of Preschoolers, Inc.), for instance, or other church and community groups.

If you are single through divorce, keep in mind that, if you and your ex are good coparents, you can complete many of the tasks just outlined by working together. Blessed are the children whose parents sacrifice their conflicts to help them mature.

A Word About Dating (page 215)

• Review the discussion about dating. What words of caution speak to you most powerfully? What changes, if any, do you need to make in your dating life or your perspective on dating and its purpose?

• Summarize in your own words the importance of not putting your child's needs into your date's hands.

Enjoy your dating life. Don't hide from your child the fact that you date. But remember that your date isn't your child's parent and won't be until and unless you marry. Keep the two processes distinct.

When to Get Help (page 216)

How do you know when you are dealing with a parenting problem that is beyond your resources? So many problems have a range of severity, and God has equipped parents to solve most problems. However, sometimes you need to contact a child therapist or specialist. Here are some guidelines to follow.

- ***Pray:*** As a parent yourself, you have some insight into how much your heavenly Father wants to help you.

    — What encouragement do you find in the truths of Proverbs 2:6 and James 1:5?

     — What current struggles, if any, do you want to bring before the Lord? Let him know that you are dependent on him and in need of his help.

- ***Stay or get connected to your child:*** Relationship with your children can help you learn information you need in order to decide how to solve problems.

    — In what context is your preschooler most likely to share what's on her heart and mind? Make a date, pray about the time in advance, and then, when you're together, listen for what your child is, and is not, saying.

     — What other adults have a close or relatively close relationship with your child? What insights do they have regarding the issue you are praying about?

- **_Always make sure your child is in ongoing medical care:_** Sometimes behavior problems are physiological in nature.

  — When was your child's last doctor's appointment or well-check?

  — What is the overall condition of your child's health? What did your pediatrician say about the problem you are concerned and praying about? Ask your doctor if you haven't already.

- **_Stay in a healthy, child-wise community:_** Being with healthy churches with good children's and youth ministries is extremely valuable to a single parent.

  — What do your child's Sunday school teachers say about your child's attitude, behaviors, and friendships? Does the director of the program have any insight or ideas about how you can help your child with the issue you're concerned about?

  — If you're not involved in a church, what research will you do this week to find out which local churches are healthy and have a thriving children's ministry for your preschooler?

- **_Deal with your desire to not be at fault:_** A great hindrance to finding out your child's problem can be your own fear of being found lacking in your parenting. Remember that all parents fall short in some way and that God heals the sick, not the well (Matthew 9:12–13).

— What lies behind your wishes to be a perfect parent? Where can you go to find healthy relationships with people who accept you, warts and all? That kind of acceptance can help you accept yourself.

— Take some time—alone with the Lord, or with a trusted friend or family member as well—to look in the mirror and honestly consider whether your parenting style is part of your child's problem. If you see that it is, then decide what you will do to change your style in order to help your child.

• **Investigate the problem as a character issue:** Explore whether the child's struggle has to do with problems with relationship, responsibility, reality, competence, talents, spiritual issues, or letting go.

— Is there a caregiver, preschool teacher, Sunday school teacher, or other significant person who can help you with the diagnosis?

— Once the character issue has been identified (if that does indeed seem to be the root of your child's problem), determine how you will deal with that issue and what you will consider signs of improvement in your child's behavior.

• **Give "character work" time to take effect:** If you are dealing with a character issue, allow the process some time.

— What does your child need to unlearn? How long has that behavior been part of the behavioral repertoire?

— Who among the adults in your child's life can join you in your effort? What might the caregiver or preschool teacher do to help this "character work" happen?

- ***Get help when all the above doesn't work over time:*** Even with the right kinds of ingredients—grace, truth, and time—some emotional and behavioral problems go beyond normal parenting resources. This is a sign to go to a specialist.

  — What resources are available to you?

  — Whom will you consult for referrals?

- ***Look for red flags that mean "get help":*** Some serious issues won't improve and may worsen until an expert intervenes. Get help quickly if you see any of the symptoms listed on pages 218–19 in the text.

  — What symptoms, if any, do you see in your child?

  — What promises from Scripture can you cling to if you see some of these red flags in your child?

Fortunately, with the right interventions, many of these issues can be resolved. Some may take much time, energy, and resources. Stay connected to your own support system and, whatever you do, stay as involved as possible with your child. Many children with serious problems grow up and out of them and establish good, productive lives because they had parents who got help in time and assisted them in working through it.

Single parenting requires much of a mom or dad. However, God is right there with appropriate resources to help you shore up the areas in which you are lacking skills, knowledge, or energy. God bless you as, with his guidance, you raise a great kid.

Hands-on Exercise

If You Do One Thing Besides Pray . . .

Take some time this week to evaluate the support system you currently have for yourself. Who can be, or perhaps already is, a partner in parenting? Who offers your child a good role model and the chance to enter the world of relationships with other people besides you? What holes do you see in your support system? What will you do to strengthen the good ties you have to people? What will you do to fill in any gaps you have identified? Prayer for the Lord's guidance and provision is always a good first step.

Folded-Hands Exercise

"My help comes from the LORD . . ."

—PSALM 121:2

Father God, I have never really thought that you understand what I deal with day and night trying to be more than I am. I find great hope in the fact that you are close to the brokenhearted and that your strength is made perfect in my human weakness.

Lord, nothing like parenting alone has made me so aware of my weakness and sin and therefore of my need for you. So I come before you, Lord, thankful that you love my child even more than I do . . . that you give wisdom when I ask . . . and that you are a Redeemer God who can help me parent my child despite this less-than-ideal situation and my very human weaknesses. Lord, I need you—and I believe you will help me each step of the way. Help my unbelief. I pray in Jesus' name. Amen.

Conclusion
When in Doubt, Connect

Parenting Principles

- Your child is also God's child—and he will not forsake his own.
- Parenting cannot be done in a vacuum; you need supporting relationships.
- When you don't know how to deal with a problem with your child, your first move is to connect with him or her.

---

*R*aising great kids is a goal that is both overwhelming and frightening for many *parents. The responsibility of having someone's life in your hands, knowing your own failings, can make anyone anxious and unsure. In addition, the amount of material we have included in this book can be daunting. You may wonder if you can do all the work on character development we have presented. We address these concerns in these final pages.*

The Divine View (page 221)

You need to understand your parenting from God's point of view.

- Remember that God chose you to be your child's parent. God chose you to be his "hands and feet" in dispensing his grace and truth to your child. He is helping, guiding, and supporting you, and he is not surprised by the twists and turns of the process. The parenting job is a large one, but not too large for you and God. He trusts you with the child he has given you, and he has equipped you for the task.

— What new idea, if any, did you find in this paragraph?

— What particular phrases do you find especially comforting and encouraging?

- Remember, too, that your child is also God's child, and he will not forsake his own (Deuteronomy 31:6, 8). God forbid that you would ever shirk your duties to your child. But even if you did, God would not leave your child unattended: "Though my father and mother forsake me, the LORD will receive me" (Psalm 27:10).

— What evidence of God's great faithfulness did you experience when you were a child?

— What specific evidence of his faithfulness to your own children have you seen?

When God calls, he enables. Nowhere will that truth be more encouraging than in your parenting.

Parents Need Support (page 222)

The Lord will indeed support your parenting efforts, but you also need the help and support of others. You can't parent well in a vacuum.

- You don't have everything your child needs, and you need to get what you don't possess from warm, honest people. You need to be in regular, vulnerable contact with people who are helping you grow not only as a parent but also personally and spiritually as an individual.

— What does your child need that you aren't able to provide? Who is helping you to fill that gap?

— Who in your life helps you grow as a parent? Who is helping you grow personally and spiritually? If your list is short or nonexistent, what will you do to get connected with warm, honest people? Be specific—and take the first step before the month is out. (The tips in the next question may help. So might our book *Safe People*. It describes how to look for and evaluate people and groups that are spiritually and emotionally good for you. Chapter 11, "Where Are the Safe People?" not only has information on good people but also a section on evaluating good churches.)

• Being a parent doesn't automatically mean you are in community. Take steps to find what resources are in your area for help with both parenting and personal/spiritual growth. Many churches now have parenting classes and fellowship groups for parents. Or you might organize friends, neighbors, or parents you meet at preschool or the day-care center to trade parenting problems and tips. If these groups are to be helpful, they need to be safe places where people can be open, that are centered on healthy parenting, and that are meeting regularly.

 — What community, if any, has becoming a parent made you a part of?

 — What support do local organizations, community programs, and churches offer you? What programs and support are available for you and your child?

Very few children have the benefit of being raised by their extended families. So, as parents, we need to supplement our efforts with the love and support of people who aren't related to us by blood.

Use the Structure (page 223)

We hope you will use this book as a road map pointing you to the six areas in which your child needs to be growing. Children can cause a lot of chaos in life, and you need to know where the parenting process is now and where it is going.

- No matter what age your child, familiarize yourself with the six character traits and address them.

  — In what ways have you already noticed these six touchstones of parenting organizing and focusing your parenting efforts? Be specific.

  — In what ways have you and your spouse enjoyed a stronger partnership since you started thinking together about these six aspects of character development?

  — What have you realized about your children since opening *Raising Great Kids*? What specific steps toward facilitating their character growth have you taken? What growth have you seen?

Again, let this book be a road map that gives you an idea of where you need to go as a parent so that your child becomes not merely a good kid, but a great kid, a kid of solid and godly character.

Normalize Failure (page 223)

You want to parent the right way, and you don't want your failures to hurt your children. The sad reality is that you have failed in the past and you will fail in the future. You can't love, provide structure for, and teach your children perfectly every time. And your failures do affect your children.

- It is much better for a child to have parents who admit failure, ask for forgiveness, and change as they learn from their errors. Be a parent who is not afraid of failure, but sees it as a way to grow. Be less afraid of mistakes and more afraid of denying them.

  — How did your own parents deal with their mistakes? What did their denial or openness teach you about failure?

  — What do you want to teach your child about failure? How do you plan to do that?

  — What does your preschooler hear from you as you encourage trial-and-error attempts to master new behaviors?

The bad news is that you will make mistakes as you parent. The good news is that children are resilient and can recover and flourish under imperfect parents.

When in Doubt, Connect (page 224)

Parenting is unpredictable because children are unpredictable. You are dealing with little human beings who are complex, impulsive, contradictory, wanting total freedom, and always in transition.

- When you don't know what to do, what do you do? This is a question all parents face.

  — When have you been at the limits of your understanding and abilities? Sleep deprivation (which often goes with the territory in this phase of parenting) makes you a prime candidate for feeling at a loss about what to do.

— "When in doubt, connect." If you followed that bit of advice intuitively in the situation you just described, what were the results? Connection never hurts, often helps, and sometimes is the entire solution to the problem.

- When a child is frustrating, provocative, and hurtful, connection may not be the first thing you think of. But connection is essential to helping your child become rooted and established in love (Ephesians 3:17).

  — Explain in your own words why relationship is the most important of all the character aspects discussed in this book. If ideas don't come easily, review the discussion of connection on pages 224–26 of the text's conclusion.

  — When you encounter an unsolvable problem, take steps to move toward your children in a way that they can experience that you are with and for them and that you want to understand their internal world. What kinds of steps could you take that would be appropriate and meaningful for your preschooler? The top of the chart (page 226 in the text) gives two examples.

Sometimes connection solves the problem, but sometimes it is only the first of many, many steps toward solving it. So teach your child by word and deed that being in relationship is very important. And may you know God's blessing as you continue to seek what is best for your child.

Hands-on Exercise

If You Do One Thing Besides Pray . . .

Choose three or four verses from Scripture that are especially encouraging to you as a parent. (Several are referred to in this chapter, and perhaps you've noticed others throughout the text.) Memorize them so that they are hidden in your heart that you might not sin against your child or the Lord (Psalm 119:11). Let them be a source of encouragement when the demands of parenting temporarily outweigh the joys.

Folded-Hands Exercise

"My help comes from the LORD . . ."

—PSALM 121:2

Heavenly Father, you chose me to be my child's parent. My child is your child as well. You will never forsake my child (Psalm 27:10)—or me, either (Deuteronomy 31:6). I can't parent well in a vacuum—and I know I shouldn't try to. I need to use this book as a road map, not a measuring stick that raps knuckles for insufficient progress. I need to admit failure to my kids, ask for forgiveness, and change as I learn from my errors. And when I am in doubt, I need to connect.

Lord, I want to take in these powerful truths as I spend time now in your presence, a presence that fills me with hope and reminds me that I am not alone in this wondrous privilege and daunting task of parenting. Enable me to be the parent you want me to be, willing to follow your example: you reconciled yourself to me first, knowing that I didn't have it in me to change until I was hooked up to you. Keep me from requiring that my child get it all together and only then make the connection. Teach me to love with a love that balances grace and truth in a way that guides my child on the path toward solid character and a life that will bring glory to you. I pray in Jesus' name. Amen.

A Special Letter to Mothers of Preschoolers

You have just completed a workbook about parenting your young child. No doubt you have found encouragement and instruction that will help you in the task of parenting.

Would you like ongoing encouragement and support? That's what MOPS is all about.

MOPS stands for Mothers of Preschoolers, a program designed for mothers with children under school age. Women in MOPS come from different backgrounds and lifestyles, yet have similar needs and a shared desire to be the best mothers they can be!

A MOPS group provides a caring, accepting atmosphere for all mothers of preschoolers. Here you have the opportunity to share concerns, explore areas of creativity, and hear instruction that will continue to equip you for the responsibilities of family and community. The MOPS program also includes MOPPETS, a loving, learning experience for children. Approximately 2,500 MOPS groups currently meet in churches in the United States and eleven other countries to meet the needs of more than 100,000 moms.

MOPS also offers

- Leadership training through resources, workshops, and mentoring. A MOPS group is led primarily by the mothers themselves, with the assistance of a MOPS mentor.
- Connection to an international network of leaders through newsletters, a radio program, conventions, and a Web site.
- A dynamic, time-tested program that has proven effective in many adaptations, including suburban, urban, teen, rural, and international settings. When you start a MOPS group, you will receive all the materials you need to begin a successful MOPS program.
- The MOPS Shop, featuring books and quality products specifically designed for mothers of preschoolers.
- An outreach ministry through the local church to mothers of preschoolers. Specially designed resources are available through MOPS for training moms in lifestyle evangelism.

To receive information such as how to join a MOPS group, or how to receive other MOPS resources such as *Mom Sense* newsletter, call or write MOPS International, P.O. Box 102200, Denver, CO 80250-2200. Phone 1-800-929-1287. E-mail: Info@MOPS.org. Web site: http://www.MOPS.org. To learn how to start a MOPS group, call 1-888-910-MOPS. For MOPS products call The MOPS Shop at 1-888-545-4040.

Name:_____

Street address:_____

City, state and ZIP Code: _____

E-mail address: _____

Phone number: _____

Are you

_____ A mom interested in joining a MOPS group?

_____ A mom interested in starting a MOPS group?

_____ A pastor or ministry leader interested in MOPS for your church?

_____ Other _____

Please mark the information you would like to receive:

_____ How to find a MOPS group near you

_____ How to start a MOPS group

_____ Complimentary issue of *Mom Sense* newsletter

_____ MOPS Shop Resource Catalog

_____ Special events announcements

Please mail to MOPS International, 1311 S. Clarkson Street, Denver, CO 80250-2200. SA95A

For information about Drs. Cloud and Townsend's books, tapes, resources, and speaking engagements, you can reach them at their Web site:

www.CloudTownsend.com

or contact

Cloud-Townsend Communications
260 Newport Center Drive #430
Newport Beach, CA 92660
Telephone: 1-800 676-HOPE
Fax: 1-949-760-1839